Praise ʃ
Do It Right the F

"I love that so many brilliant experts came together to share their wisdom in *Do It Right the First Time*. The publishing industry can be overwhelming, but this book will help writers navigate the terrain and avoid many common mistakes. Bravo!"
—Stephanie Chandler, CEO, Nonfiction Authors Association

"*Do It Right the First Time: How to Write, Publish, and Market Your Bestseller* is a powerful anthology filled with tips, tricks, and techniques from industry experts who want only the best for your publishing experience."
—Jill Lublin, 4x best-selling author, international speaker, and master publicity strategist

"We started our author journey through self-publishing, a credible way to get your words into the world. With proper guidance, you can create a professional product that enhances your brand and delivers your message to the readers you serve. Valerie J. Lewis Coleman is a knowledgeable and skilled mentor who helps writers launch the best possible print and digital products. Many writers will benefit from the guidance she generously shares."
—Mindy Kiker and Jennifer Kochert, FlourishWriters co-founders

Other books in the
Do It Right Series...

Publish and Market Your Bestseller
- Strategies to save thousands of dollars, hours of research, and tons of frustration
- Little-known secrets to get your books to readers
- Ways to generate multiple streams of income
- Proven resources to accelerate your success

Conversations with Marketing Experts
- Sound legal advice for copyrights, contracts, and collaborations
- The 5Cs of generating six figures from your book
- Strategies to leverage your expertise with Amazon, podcasts, and the media

Do It Right the First Time Workbook
With the volume of information shared in the three-book series, readers requested a workbook to capture aha moments, amazing discoveries, and action items. This spiral-bound book has questions, quotes, and quill space for you to move forward with your book projects. DoItTheFirstTime.com

For Kindle eBooks, visit https://amzn.to/3zeQ51j.

Do It Right the First Time:

Write Your Bestseller

Compiled by

Valerie J. Lewis Coleman

Published by
Pen of the Writer
PenOfTheWriter.com
Englewood, OH

Published by

Pen of the Writer
Englewood, OH
PenOfTheWriter.com

Library of Congress Control Number: 2022914273

ISBN-13: 979-8-9865108-0-4

Edited by Valerie J. Lewis Coleman of PenOfTheWriter.com and Sharahnne Gibbons of SomethingInComma.com

Printed in the United States of America

Table of Contents

Introduction

I am excited to serve you on your publishing journey with advice from over thirty experts. Combined, we have hundreds of years of industry experience to help you master self-publishing to make money. We want you to succeed.

For your convenience, this series is divided into the three major aspects of publishing: writing, publishing, and marketing. No matter where you are in the process, you will gain information, insight, and inspiration to accelerate your progress.

To further catapult your success, consolidate your notes, and capture your action items, the *Do It Right the First Time Workbook* complements the series with questions, quotes, and quilling space to capture the nuggets you plan to implement. Get your copy at DoItTheFirstTime.com.

May your fingers dance across the keyboard and your pen glide across the paper as the world makes room for your gift.

Valerie J. Lewis Coleman

Valerie J. Lewis Coleman

Write Your Bestseller

"Start writing no matter what. The water does not flow until the faucet is turned on."

—Louis L'Amour

Valerie J. Lewis Coleman

The Real Reason
Your Book is Not Finished

Valerie J. Lewis Coleman

Has anyone ever told you that you have a powerful story and need to write a book? Are you so proficient at something that people often ask you to explain how to do it? Do you feel compelled to write a book to help others on their journey? Whatever the impetus, God has purpose for your passion and pain.

Which of these responses best describes where you are in the writing process?

1. My manuscript is done!
2. I have a few chapters complete.
3. I have ideas written on notepads, napkins, and toilet paper.
4. I have ideas floating around in my head.
5. Jesus, be a fence! I have absolutely no clue what to write or how to write it.

In my experience with clients—and myself—I identified the top three reasons your book is not finished. To remedy the dilemma, biblical principles and practical tools are provided to generate forward momentum. Pen ready? These are the top three reasons:

1. Fear, which is often rooted in family, friends, and finances.

2. Focus, which is hindered by commotions, chaos, and confusion.
3. Forgiveness, it's actually unforgiveness; however, for the *f* alliteration and ease of remembering, forgiveness works better.

These strategies to eradicate fear, engage focus, and exercise forgiveness are transferable beyond writing and can be applied to other aspects of your life.

Fear

Have you ever asked yourself any of these self-sabotaging questions?

- Is my book good enough?
- Am I good enough?
- Am I an imposter?
- How will my family feel about me publishing my story...which may implicate them?
- Will my family forgive me for telling my truth?
- Can I be sued?
- Do I have enough pages?
- Can I afford to publish this book?

Let me address your concerns about these questions from the spiritual perspective.

- The enemy comes to steal your peace, kill your dreams, and destroy your destiny (John 10:10); however, faith and fear cannot occupy the same space. Since faith without works is dead (James 2:26), replace that fear with faith and put action with it.

- God has not given you the spirit of fear, but of power, love, and a sound mind (2 Timothy 1:7).
- Proverbs 23:7 states "As a man thinks in his heart, so is he." Transform your thinking to things that are true, honest, just, pure, lovely, and good (Philippians 4:8).

Even if you're concerned about how your family will react to your book—like many of my clients— follow these suggestions:

- Write the first draft as if no one will ever read it. Get it out to purge and purify your emotional attachment. The uncensored version is therapeutic and gives you confidence to keep writing.
- Be transparent about your truth. This step will help you—and your readers— experience genuine transformation.
- Refine it for publishing by hiring professional editors.

On the practical side...

An extensive study determined that 85% of the things test subjects worried about never happened.[1]

---

[1]Goewey, Joseph, *85 Percent of What We Worry About Never Happens*, HuffPost.com, online:

For the 15% that did happen, 79% of the participants discovered they handled the situation better than expected, or the experience taught them a valuable lesson. As a result, a whopping 97% of what you worry about is nothing more than a "fearful mind punishing you with exaggerations and misperceptions."

The biggest hurdle for most people is managing the six inches between their ears. Let's start shifting your mindset and changing your perception by redefining FEAR. Instead of defining F-E-A-R as Finding Excuses And Reasons, try these alternatives:

- False Evidence Appearing Real
- Feeling Excited And Ready
- Face Everything And Rise
- F_____ E_____ A_____ R_____
- F_____ E_____ A_____ R_____
- F_____ E_____ A_____ R_____

Encourage yourself with I-am affirmations that you write, speak, and believe until they manifest.

- "I am inspiring, encouraging, and empowering people with my message."
- "I am transforming lives."
- "I am experiencing transformation."
- "I am a best-selling author."
- "I am _____."
- "I am _____."

---

https://www.huffpost.com/entry/85-of-what-we-worry-about_b_8028368. Accessed online 12.15.20.

You're probably aware of goal setting, but have you heard of fear setting? Tim Ferriss created a seven-step approach to work through fear.[2]

1. Define your fear about finishing your book.
2. What can you do to prevent or repair damage?
3. What are the benefits (internal and external) of finishing your book?
4. In the unlikely event your fear comes true, how can you get back on track?
5. What are you avoiding due to fear?
6. What is the lack of action costing you financially, emotionally, and physically?
7. Why are you still waiting?

Do it scared! Take the leap! Do at least one thing you fear every day to finish your book. Trust that God will catch you or you'll sprout wings and fly!

Focus

The enemy uses fear and distractions as weapons to get you off track. His fiery darts include chaos, clutter, and confusion; all of which are creativity blockers.

If you started writing and got stuck, it may be that you're trying to edit (left brain) when you should

---

[2]Ferriss, Tim, *Fear Setting: The Most Valuable Exercise I Do Every Month*, Tim.Blog, online: https://tim.blog/2017/05/15/fear-setting. Accessed online 12.15.20.

be writing (right brain). James 1:8 says that a double-minded man is unstable in all his ways. Do not edit (aka backspace, delete, erase) because you shift hemispheres from right-brain creativity to left-brain critical thinking. The result is often frustration because your creativity is stifled.

To help with focus, eliminate distractions. Get clear on the who, what, where, when, and why of your writing. Write your vision, make it plain, and run with it (Habakkuk 2:2) by identifying the following elements:

- To **whom** you're writing. Be specific about your ideal reader. Create an avatar considering demographics and psychographics (habits, needs, wants, pain points).
- **What** message do you want to share? What problem do you solve? What is the moral of your story?
- **Where** is the best place for you to write? Your home and/or workplace may not be good locations to pen your manuscript. I prefer a "third place" with access to restrooms, food, and Wi-Fi.
- **When** is the best time for you to write? If you're an early riser, get up a few minutes before the house awakes. If you're most creative at midday, write during your lunch break and save calories.
- **Why** are you writing? Is your objective to change lives, document family history, or

leave a legacy for your children? Do you want to grow your business, attract more clients, or generate revenue? Note that your why can encompass several options.

Get clarity on how your message will change your readers. Someone's life depends on you finishing your book. Dr. Myles Monroe said that the richest place in the world is the graveyard because people die without sharing their gifts and talents. The Earth is groaning for the manifestation of your gift.

Practical Focus Tools
- Create a vision board identifying the who, what, where, when, and why for your book. Display it in a conspicuous area so you see it every day. If you have a cover concept and working title, add those as visual reminders of your book.
- You cannot make time, but you can prioritize it. Schedule time to write. Start with small daily goals like 15 minutes or 100 words, and then expand as you feel comfortable. Email me at info@penofthewriter.com for the Pen of the Writer Weekly Planning Calendar and Write Your Bestseller Checklist to assist you with scheduling and adhering to writing your bestseller.
- Organize your thoughts to relieve the clutter in your mind. Use a composition book, voice

recorder, or your smartphone for immediate capture of ideas and inspirations.

- Declutter your writing space. Fill it with your favorite colors, tabletop fountain or sound machine (water is an amazing conduit for creativity), and calming scents like eucalyptus, lavender, and cloves.

Forgiveness... or the lack thereof

After fear, harboring unforgiveness is the top creativity blocker. Matters left unresolved can grow like a deep-rooted weed causing resentfulness, bitterness, and physical ailments. Not forgiving is like drinking poison and expecting the other person to die. How's that working for you?

Clench your fists so tight that your nails leave indentations in your palms. Are you clenching? Like the virtual brick wall or other defense mechanisms used to protect yourself, unforgiveness is like a clenched fist that keeps out "stuff." But it also holds you hostage. You cannot give or receive when your hands—and heart—are closed.

Forgiveness transforms anger and hurt into healing and peace. Forgiveness can help you overcome depression, anxiety, and rage. Forgiveness gives you the power to resolve personal and relational conflicts. When you make a conscious decision to release a grudge, hurt, or disappointment, you take control, stand in your power, and own your worth.

Forgiveness is not for the other person; it's for you. Let me be clear, you do not have to confront the offender to offer forgiveness. You can verbally forgive them...from a distance. You can write a letter and then burn it. You can pray for them. Whatever you do, make forgiveness a lifestyle. Email me at info@penofthewriter.com for resources I use and share with clients to help free our minds to operate in forgiveness.

Now, write! Write about why you cannot write. Write forgiveness letters. Write what you know. Write your bestseller!

Best-selling author and award-winning publisher, Valerie J. Lewis Coleman serves professional speakers and experts to magnify and monetize their message by publishing quality books. With over fifteen years of experience in the book business, she has published over 170 authors and helped thousands of writers navigate the challenges of self-publishing. This expert divulges industry secrets on avoiding the top five mistakes made by 95% of new authors, pricing your book to sell, and identifying shady publishers. Valerie hosts citywide book events, which have connected over 700 authors to avid readers. Her dynamic presentation and knowledge of the business take writers from pen to paper to published as they master self-publishing to make money! Schedule a complimentary discovery session with Valerie at https://penofthewriter.as.me.

Connect with Valerie
PenOfTheWriter.com
Amazon.com/author/valeriejlewiscoleman
Facebook.com/PenOfTheWriter
LinkedIn.com/in/PenOfTheWriter
Instagram.com/PenOfTheWriter
Twitter.com/PenOfTheWriter

Valerie's Favorite Resource
A weekly planning calendar. At a glance, I can review, revise, and replicate my efforts to be more effective (doing the right thing) and efficient (doing the thing right).

_____

_____

_____

_____

_____

_____

_____

_____

_____

_____

_____

_____

_____

_____

_____

_____

_____

_____

_____

From Dream to Manuscript: Strategies to Jumpstart Your Writing Career

Chavonne D. Stewart, Ph.D.

An unexpected event and the actions of a curious six-year-old child stemmed a story that I had to tell the world. The details of my adventure are captured in my first book, *The Lie*.

Dream to Manuscript

"Only dreams believed become dreams achieved."
— Author Unknown

Do you believe that you can achieve your dream of writing your manuscript? My answer to you, "Yes, you can."

More than thirty years later, I penned my first book. Thank goodness I had a great memory. Like many others, I was affected by the economic crash of 2008. With my job gone, I had time to focus on writing.

I began by developing my characters and the plot that supported my climatic childhood event. For my main character, I chose Amilya as the first name because a favorite childhood book was *Amelia Bedelia*. Since rose is my favorite flower, I added it to her name: Amilya Rose.

A dear friend and mentor who I worked with in Christian education taught me to tweak what I was doing instead of reinventing wheels. I looked at books and cartoons for children. At the time, Dora the Explorer was the hottest kids' character. I wanted kids to go on adventures with Amilya Rose. I wanted her to be fun, smart, and African American. I do not recall reading any children's books with characters that reflected me on the cover. I wanted Amilya Rose to have a diverse group of friends to teach kids love and appreciation of other ethnicities. Other important factors included showing a godly family structure with a father and mother. I wanted the books to entertain while teaching life lessons, so each book concludes with Amilya Rose reflecting on the journey.

Strategies to Jumpstart Your Writing

Create a book vision board as a visual reminder of what you want to achieve. The board is used to layout elements of your book including setting, plot, characters, climax, and conflict. You may choose a more elaborate board with vivid pictures and descriptive words. Your board can be a simple story synopsis that conveys the narrative arc, the problem or plot, the character, and how the book ends. Display it on your office wall or writing nook. Take a picture of it to carry with you.

Some writers prefer handwriting to composing on a computer. Some people write best using an outline, while others take a less-structured approach. Another method to put to paper is brain dumping. Without concern for grammar, spelling errors, or order of events, you write everything that comes to mind. Do not edit. That phase comes later.

Keep a journal with you because you never know when inspiration will strike. When school supplies go on sale, stock up on spiral notebooks, composition books, and other writing supplies. Technology offers many tools: voice recorders, Google's speech-to-text, and free online writing tools like Reedsy.com.

I write best in silence, so late at night, when the house is quiet, is best for me. You may like noise in the background like soft music or the television. When do you get a surge of creative energy? Trial and error may be your friend when determining what's best for you.

Your writing should be attention-grabbing. If necessary, refresh yourself on writing devices like alliteration, similes, metaphors, sensory details, and onomatopoeia.

Know and understand the genre you are writing. It makes a difference in how your story is patterned, your ideal readers, and marketing. If you are writing historical fiction set in the 19th century, televisions should not be in your story. Research before you start writing and avoid Wikipedia as a resource because anyone can add unverified information.

If your English could use a refresher, or you need motivation/encouragement, join a writing group. Find writing associations in your community or state. If you are located in Georgia, consider joining the Georgia Writers Association (GeorgiaWriters.org). Although the cost is minimal, participate so you don't waste your money.

Your publisher or editor may have suggestions for retreats to stay connected and help develop your writing. I attended Free Your Mind Writers Retreat (FreeYourMindWritersRetreat.com) hosted by Pen of the Writer. I gained great tips on how to market my books.

Some other points to consider as you write your bestseller:

- Don't rely on memory. Write your thoughts, inspirations, and ideas so you don't forget them.
- Purchase a fireproof safe to store notes, journals, and hardcopies of your manuscript.
- Backup your work to a flash drive, external hard drive, and the cloud.
- Add the date to the file name each time you save your manuscript. For example, Do_It_Right_070722.doc This strategy keeps multiple versions of your book as another backup plan and provides access to accidentally deleted content.
- Grammar is important. Use the spell check feature in your word processor. Google is your friend, but it does not hurt to purchase a

dictionary and thesaurus. Grammarly.com is a virtual writing assistant that helps with spelling, punctuation, plagiarism, and more.

- Invest in your vision. Hire a professional editor who is proficient in your genre. Understand the level of editing they perform—content editing, copy editing, or proofreading—their fee structure—by the word, page, or hour—and expected completion date. Take time searching for the right editor as you will partner with them to bring your vision to light. Your manuscript is your baby, and like every good parent, we take exceptional care of our babies.
- Do not be offended by constructive criticism. It helps you grow as a writer.

Take a deep breath. Start by writing fifteen minutes at a time; advice given to me. You will see measurable progress. You can do it!

Shoulda! Coulda! Woulda!

Entrepreneurship was not new to me because I worked as a part-time hairstylist. However, my journey to authorpreneur (author + entrepreneur) had challenges as I stepped into unfamiliar territory.

I had several shoulda-coulda-woulda moments; things I wish I knew before I jumped into the book business. My greatest challenge occurred after the manuscript was complete. As I researched how to publish, I learned that traditional publishing was a complicated process and self-publishing was not as affordable as I expected. My book sat on the shelf a couple more years.

I am responsible for all aspects of my business. Since book production has many elements, I contracted service providers with "assumed" proficiency in my areas of weakness. I wish I understood the value of having expert guidance at the beginning of this process. I highly recommend that you hire a mentor to help you navigate publishing. Someone who has experience as an authorpreneur, done what you desire to do, and has results to prove it. A good mentor will keep you on track with support and accountability, which equals empowerment and motivation. I wanted to be a best-selling author who generated a seven-figure income. I had vision; however, connecting with someone early in the process could have saved me money, time, and frustration.

Research editors. You want someone with experience in your genre and whom others speak well of. I had a good editor and made the mistake of allowing someone else edit my story. She spoke negatively of the first editor. I'm not sure if she tried to get my business by badmouthing her competition, but I don't think she offers editing services anymore.

I found an illustrator on Craigslist. Initially, he seemed to be on the up-and-up. I paid a deposit to start the project. He sent a few sketches of Amilya Rose and then stopped communicating with me. My gut told me to cut ties and I did without hesitating. I lost about $100, but the lesson had value far beyond that. I now rely on recommendations. One author recommended <u>Fiverr.com</u>. It's a site of freelancers who provide all kinds of services perfect for entrepreneurs. I use Fiverr for banners, book cover designs, and illustrations. Since providers do not receive payment until you approve their work, you have a level of protection from fraud.

Marketing is a key factor to your success. I am not a fan of marketing because it is not my forte, but I needed clarity on how to build and establish my brand. Until you master marketing, invest in an individual or team to help you. If your goal is to sell tons of books, you can become discouraged. This process takes time. Be intentional and consistent with your messaging. I learned to use social media for marketing and networking. I joined groups for writers, business owners, and children's book authors. Prior to COVID-19, I attended in-person events to market and sell my product.

I recommend Dan Poynter's book, *Self-Publishing Manual Volumes 1 & 2*. To save money, I borrowed it from the public library. Speaking of libraries, connect with your local branch. They offer classes and opportunities to promote your book. If you want to do a book release or reading, room rental is inexpensive. Get connected! Stay connected! You will see the fruit of your labor.

Chavonne D. Stewart, Ph.D. is an accomplished self-published author, coach, and speaker. *The Adventures of Amilya Rose* children's series published by Dogwood Farms Publications birthed her author journey. She has written and published five books and contributed to anthologies: *Dear Depression* and *L3: Learn, Love, Lead*. Chavonne is a coach and facilitator who conducts leadership training and development to help organizations thrive. She is the host and creator of DNA of Diversity Podcast. Chavonne earned a doctorate in leadership studies at Beulah Heights University. She holds an MS in management from Troy University, a BA in history from Kennesaw State University, and a life-coach certification through DreamReleaser Coaching, LLC. She enjoys traveling, shopping, reading, and spending time with family.

Connect with Chavonne
ChavonneStewart.com
Amazon.com/~/e/B00SZMX0XE
Linkedin.com/in/chavonnestewart
Instagram.com/chavonned.stewart
Twitter.com/chavonnestewart

Chavonne's Favorite Resource
TheCreativePenn.com because it provides tips and resources that inspire and assist those new to the writing process or desiring to reignite their passion.

Finding the Right Way to Write Your Story

Leeta Song

Have you ever thought about how much power is in a book? Many answers to life's challenges can be found on the pages of books. You read for many different reasons:

- To learn about a subject
- To escape your reality
- To find comfort
- To relate

Think about the best book you've ever read. What did you enjoy about it? What made you say, "Now *that* is a good book"? Whether you read for entertainment or to gain knowledge, your experience with literature gives you a gift. With each book read, you grow as a person, learn information to share with others, and possibly make life-altering decisions. How amazing is that? But what about your story? Have you ever thought about how much your story can influence someone who reads it?

My writing journey led me to discover 157 books within me. Publishing them at the same time was not a good idea because each book deserves its own spotlight. Many people think they do not have a story worth sharing, but I'm here to tell you that you absolutely do. Your story might be the reason someone finds the solution to a difficult problem. Perhaps your story empowers someone in a way they never felt before.

I've read many books, but not every book spoke to me. Authors have unique writing styles that speak to people differently. Depending on the need, your message will resonate more than someone who shares a similar story. Everyone's story has a purpose, and everyone's story speaks to someone. For that reason, you have to write and share your story.

Your pain, suffering, and mayhem are treasured gems that allow you to learn and eventually teach others. However, oftentimes people put the gems in a chest and throw them into the ocean. Your challenges have equipped you with knowledge and courage. With firsthand experience, you hold the blueprint that will help someone travel the path you've already walked. It's time to write your book! Someone needs your story to navigate their journey. Your story is the key to unlock someone's peace, profit, or passion. Let's go on an adventure to find those hidden treasures. Don't waste any more time waiting to birth the powerful story inside of you.

Brain Dump

Brain dumping helps to clear your head. Write everything that comes to mind without thinking, questioning, or stopping to correct it. Your sole purpose is to get your thoughts out of your head and onto an index card, notepad, or journal. When you can't write any more, highlight similar ideas, and then rewrite them on a new piece of paper. You will be surprised at the buried treasure you find, and you may discover content for several chapters.

Keyboard Freestyle

Another technique is to sit at your computer. Meditate and pray about what story you should bring forth into this world. Close your eyes, place your fingers on the keyboard in the proper positions, and let the ideas flow. Type as long as you can without stopping, deleting, or backspacing. Those are editing functions that halt creativity. Let your imagination run wild. You may feel like you're straying away from the main idea, but that's okay. Keep typing. You might be surprised at how this freestyle technique has a way of coming full circle, or helping you navigate places where you once struggled. Maybe you got stuck developing a character. Your free-flowing freestyle session can take you to an incredible place of quirks, mannerisms, and motivators that add layers to your character. That's what freestyle writing is about: freedom. Freedom leads to discovery, and discovery creates great material that takes your readers on an amazing journey. If you're fascinated, they will be, too. When you don't have anything else to type, cut and paste similar ideas together.

Dictation

If you're not good at handwriting or typing, dictation is your best bet. You speak into a device, and programs like Otter.ai or Dragon Dictation transcribe your words. Once everything is transcribed, rearrange the information into categories. You'll notice patterns forming. For example, you may have significantly more information in one category compared to another which could indicate one of the following opportunities:

- The "greater" category will be a chapter.
- The "greater" category is too broad. Divide it into subcategories to create additional chapters.
- More research is needed to gather content for the "lesser" category.

These observations will help sharpen your skills so you can grow as a writer. The more you use this technique, the more you solidify your style of writing.

Chapter Construction

Using these treasure-hunting techniques, it's not uncommon to experience anxiety or information overload. You may have content for several chapters or multiple books. If you need to relax your mind, take a break. Come back to the story refreshed so you can attack your work from a better perspective.

Some authors write in chronological order. Others have a basic outline but skip around to write the chapter that is top of mind. Choose the method that's best for you and then add details to make your story cohesive. If you find that one chapter is not as sharp as you want, or you're not satisfied, move to another chapter.

Avoid getting sidetracked with new ideas that are unrelated to your book. I am no stranger to this distraction. When it happens, jot the thoughts on a separate sheet of paper to reference later. This step is critical for two reasons:

1. You don't want those nagging thoughts diverting you from your current project.
2. Those ideas might come in handy later in this book or another one.

Since this draft is your first, it doesn't have to be perfect. Enjoy the flow of capturing more gems.

Project Clarity

To move you closer to completion, answer these questions for clarity on your project:

- What is your book topic? This question is important because you may know what you want to write and still be all over the place. Many times, writers are too general. Have you ever asked someone what their book is about, and it takes them a few minutes to explain? Don't be that person. Know exactly what your topic is and be able to explain it in thirty seconds. This elevator pitch will go a long way when it comes to promoting and selling your book. If you can't easily tell someone what your book is about, why would they want to read it?

- What story speaks to your purpose? Which one most pulls on your heartstrings or which one are you most passionate about sharing? Which story shows your transformation from the greatest pain you experienced and can help readers on their journey?

- What solution or result do you provide your readers? What is the quick win for your audience? What subject can you talk about with the least amount of effort? What questions can you correctly answer to give readers direction, insight, or encouragement? What is your expertise? What do you want people to remember about you? Authors are problem solvers, so think about the "aha!" moments you want your readers to experience.

- Why does your story matter? It is your job to explain how your book benefits readers. Will it entertain them? Will it encourage, inspire, or motivate? Will it guide them step-by-step to a sought-out place? Why is your story so important that another person will want to read it? Be clear about your message and how it serves readers.

- Who is your ideal reader? Be specific about who you want to read your book. Is your message to a younger version of you who wished this book was available years ago? Deep dive into the personality, qualities, and habits of your ideal reader like you are creating a character for a novel. The more specific the reader profile you create, the better you will be at finding your readers, presenting your story, and making a difference.

- When is a good time to publish? Some people chase market trends, while others create a legacy with information that can be read for generations. Timeless.

- Why is now the time to publish this story? Answer this question with passion. Is your *now* because you are ready to stop holding back? Is your *now* because you have courage to share your story so others can learn from you? Your why is just as important as your what. Your why will keep you up at night writing new material. Your why is the reason you will publish your book. Your why creates amazing power and momentum.

- What is your projected deadline? Set a date to work toward but be flexible. Many factors go into effective publishing, so your deadline may change.

By keeping stories inside you, you do a disservice for the people meant to read it. No matter if it's fiction, nonfiction, or a memoir, your story is needed. Don't let anything hold you back. Every story has gems that can light someone's darkness or be the sound for someone's silence. Speak up. Write your story. Show up in the most powerful way and ignite someone who wants to be heard, seen, and believed. You have the power to inspire others. Are you going to use it?

As an inspirational speaker and book publishing coach, Leeta Song's passion is helping others bring clarity to their publishing goals. She helps authors discover the treasures within their untold stories to make a difference in the world. Having overcome poverty and adversity, she co-runs several family businesses. Despite life's twists and turns, she never let go of her youthful dream to become an author. Her path of discovery led her to the philosophy that your greatest pain, suffering, and mayhem are gifts; life lessons that teach resiliency and build character. She believes that sharing stories of healing and triumph is important because you never know who you can help.

Stay tuned for *Awaken the Purpose Within: Uncovering Your Passion to Live a Life You Love*.

Connect with Leeta
Amazon.com/Leeta-Song/e/B00R33RP3C
Facebook.com/leeta.author
Linkedin.com/in/leetasong
Instagram.com/leeta_song

Leeta's Favorite Resource
Otter.ai because you can speak your story to transcribe it. They offer 600 minutes free every 30 days.

_____

_____

_____

_____

_____

_____

_____

_____

_____

_____

_____

_____

_____

_____

_____

_____

_____

_____

_____

Create Your Own Writing Experience

Lorri Lewis

"When are you going to write a book?"
"What's your book about?"
"Girl, what's taking you so long?"

I've been bombarded with these questions for as long as I remember. As an English educator, I have been perceived to have writing talents that could churn out books at a moment's notice. How wrong my "fans" have been!

I've been writing since I was sixteen years old. I spent hours at my typewriter creating stories full of details and dialogue between high school "lovers." However, it wasn't until the pandemic sat me down that I felt compelled to write my first book. I soon realized that writing was much easier than the publishing route I chose.

I love to read and not just because it's part of my day job. I've been reading since I was three years old, but as I immersed myself in professional organizations and networked with educators from around the country, my interest in the writing craft grew beyond reading a good story and writing articles. I analyzed the author's writing style, the structure of the work, the characters' meaningful and realistic qualities, the setting, plot, and more. I wanted to know why and how books came to fruition and how some were adapted into movies. As a result, my writing journey became a study of the art of writing and how it becomes worthy of publication.

In 2010, a colleague introduced me to *Bird by Bird: Some Instructions on Writing and Life* by Anne Lamott, a resource I recommend every aspiring author read. It's about trusting yourself and making daily advances to birth your narrative. The book reinforces that every writer's journey is different but taking those daily steps "bird-by-bird" will lead you to birth that work whether fiction or nonfiction. I read *On Writing: A Memoir of the Craft* by Stephen King. I had no expectations of this book furthering my goal of becoming a writer; however, it was a joyous, humorous experience. It provided an enlightening perspective on how a writer developed into a renowned author who influences millions of readers. It helped propel me to complete my first book.

I was surrounded by individuals who encouraged me and provided resources to get it done. I finished writing in approximately six weeks. However, the best advice and what got me started with *7 Must Dos Before I Do: Making Wedding Planning Memorable and Easy* came from a fellow educator and motivational speaker in Wisconsin, Chris Clarke-Epstein.

From attending one of her writing seminars, I began the process by taking the following steps. I invite you to do the same.

- Complete these sentence starters:
  - o I want to write this book because... (describe your WHY)
  - o I want to write a book to... (describe the results you want for readers)
  - o The major reason this book won't happen is... (describe your fears)
- Identify your ideal reader. To whom are you writing this book? Be specific.
- Visit a local bookstore to see what's already published in your subject. Take note of titles, table of contents, number of pages, graphics, color, back cover, etc. What's going to make your book stand out from these?
- Create several working titles.
- Keep a notebook/journal with you at all times. You never know when something or someone will inspire new content and you don't want to forget it.
- Create a chart that breaks your content into sections. For a visual of what needs to be eliminated or combined, refer to the chart on page 49. This chart—a living document that changes throughout your writing journey—helps keep you organized. Note: These columns pertain to self-help/nonfiction books; however, they can be modified for fiction.

- Introduction. How do you want to "introduce" your topic and/or story? Write a brief overview of what the reader can expect to learn.
- Topic. What's the central theme for each chapter?
- Quote. Do you have a quote from another source that connects to this chapter? If so, capture the quote and who said it.
- Essay. What specific points do you want to cover in this chapter?
- Task. What action should your reader take after reading this chapter?
- Summary. What are the main takeaways your reader should garner from this chapter?
- Suggested Reading List. Include a list of titles that inspired your book or provide more detail about your topic.

We all have a good story inside of us. I can coach anyone through the writing process, but my most valuable suggestion is to find what works best for you. Many dedicate a certain number of hours per day to writing. My best writing occurs when I set weekly goals and dedicate time to write. For added motivation, I reward myself for successes no matter how small. If you experience droughts or writer's block, step aside and take a moment away from writing. Many suggest carrying a journal or notebook, which is great advice. With technology, you can record voice memos and notes on your smart device. A dedicated writing space is another great suggestion, but if you're like me, you get bored easily and need a change in scenery for inspiration. Don't lock yourself into what others deem essential. Create your own writing experience.

One of my favorite parts of the process was sharing the final draft with others. Although I was nervous, I felt exhilarated about being done and letting others react to the finished product. I chose the following individuals to read and provide feedback:

- Someone who didn't know I was writing a book and was unfamiliar with its content
- Someone who represented my ideal reader
- A grammarian who gave syntactical, mechanical, and rhetorical feedback
- A former client who had gone through my wedding-planning process. She had a personal connection to the book's content and played the role of wedding-planning alumnus.

In selecting your beta readers, choose one or two people from each of the categories.

Once I completed this stage, I was ready to start the self-publishing process. I created an account with Kindle Direct Publishing (KDP.Amazon.com) to publish my physical copy and eBook on Amazon. I used IngramSpark.com for wider distribution of both formats and things became most challenging. I had issues with the cover file because it was incorrectly formatted. Despite having a cover done by a Fiverr freelancer, I had to enlist another graphic designer to create a new cover per IngramSpark's recommendation. I had issues with the eBook file, which also had to be reformatted.

I don't think I will choose the do-it-yourself route again. I considered Book Baby; however, their pricing was higher than my budget. In the end, I spent almost the same amount because of the issues I had to reconcile, redo, and repay.

Do lots of research. Resources like books, podcasts, and seminars can give you more information than you want or need. You'd be surprised at what you can learn. While listening to a podcast about self-publishing, I learned how books make it to *The New York Times* bestseller list, and it's not readership.

Set a budget to produce your book and incorporate a pre-release campaign to generate money before the book drops. I love that I can purchase wholesale copies from IngramSpark to sell or gift to potential clients. At the same time, the general public can purchase copies from Amazon.

What I experienced hasn't deterred me from doing it again. I'm working on my first novel, and I can't wait for you to read it!

Lorri's Content Chart

Introduction				
Chapter	Topic	Quote	Essay	Task
1				
2				
3				
4				
5				
Summary				
Suggested Reading List				

Lorri Lewis has served Michigan couples as a wedding planner for over two decades. Affectionately known as The DirectHer, she's been a featured writer in the Bridal section of *The Jewish News*, *Detroit Wedding Day Magazine*, and *The Michigan Chronicle*. She was recognized as one of the Top 10 Successful Women Entrepreneurs of Color by Fundera, Inc. and is a founding member of The National Society of Black Event and Wedding Professionals. When she is not wedding planning, she's recruiting and honing talent in her high school English classes, serving as a wedding coordinator at her church, and hosting her weekly podcast, *Before the Big Day*.

Connect with Lorri
TheDirectHer.com
Amazon.com/author/lorrilewis
Facebook.com/thedirecther
Linkedin.com/in/thedirecther
Instagram.com/directherweddings

Lorri's Favorite Resource
Bird by Bird: Some Instructions on Writing and Life by Anne Lamot. Every time I read it; I gain a different outlook to believe in myself as a writer. I have something to contribute to the world, and so do you.

The Write Way to My Destiny

Jeri D. Dokes

In 1978, I was a freshman in high school when the album, *Destiny*, hit the charts. As the musical group known as The Jackson 5, belted out the chorus of the title track, I sang along with the feelings of desire the lyrics portrayed. I wanted destiny like they did...designed just for me.

My love for reading and writing poetry led to a lifestyle and career focused around communication and language expression.

"I found my freedom. Writing is my destiny!"

Growing up on a farm in rural northeast Ohio, community activities and resources for a young Black family were scarce. So, when the traveling salesman from *World Book Encyclopedia* came knocking, my parents, Roosevelt and Doris Jackson, wrote the check. Thumbing through the pages of book one of *Childcraft-The How and Why Library*, I found one whimsical picture after another of frolicking children or grazing field animals. Gaily colored illustrations of fun, excitement, and sometimes pain, were expressed in the words of the authors. I read nursery rhymes, often reading them multiple times. Poems caught my attention, too. Enjoying the rhythm of the rhymes, I took in all of it. For my primary years, reading was my music.

By age nine, I had written, as my brother, Roosevelt, Jr. often teased, *My Book of Poems*. Something about the way I proudly enunciated and claimed my poems tickled him. I kept my handwritten collection of personally illustrated works in a green notebook. I read them aloud to anyone who would listen.

After I graduated from high school, the notebook was set aside, possibly in a box, sadly never to be seen again. The memories of my first unpublished work remain in my heart and mind. A sense of motivation to this day.

I studied communication and journalism at the University of Akron. I worked at the television studio and wrote for the campus newspaper. I wrote an article about the decreasing retention of Black students at the college. Dr. Sebetha Jenkins (Jenkins-Leggette at that time) was the director of minority affairs. It was a great opportunity to interview someone in an administrative position...who looked like me! Dr. Jenkins congratulated me on the published story and insisted that we stay in touch. Her mentorship and personal support inspired me to keep writing.

After graduating from college, I wrote and edited for community newspapers in Indianapolis, Indiana and Dayton, Ohio. My sister, Janet, told me that *The Dayton Defender* newspaper needed writers. As the publisher of the sole source of news and information for the Black community, Mr. Ernie Bickerstaff operated on a small budget. Like most freelance writers, I was paid per story. Mr. Bickerstaff assigned me to interview top city officials including Mayor Richard Clay Dixon and Ohio representative for Dayton, C.J. McLin, Jr. In 1988, I interviewed Reverend Jesse Jackson during his presidential campaign. I interviewed Earl Graves, Sr., publisher of *Black Enterprise* magazine and actor, Fred "The Hammer" Williamson. I wrote feature stories of local athletes and school board decisions. The variety of stories gave me experience that built my confidence in writing.

As a middle-grade English teacher, one of the essential skills taught to students is mastering writing. In addition to writing narratives, my students researched topics of interest while learning to support their writing with legitimate sources and appropriate citations. As I graded essays and reports, it brought back memories of the joys of writing. With a slight nudge from my youngest sister, Jina, I was encouraged to move forward with my writing.

Upon reflection, I realized that I never stopped writing poetry. I write poetry for specific occasions or on a whim. I am learning to grab a pen and paper when I wake up with thoughts that resemble a story or poem. A few have been lost because I assumed that I would remember the story screaming in my head. I often share pieces with my family or close friends for approval. That's my way of checking for value since I no longer get paid to write.

A consistent theme in my work is sentiment.

When my mother's younger brother died, she asked me to "write something." *My Brother, My Brother, My Friend,* is about my Uncle Ronald. I wrote a poem to celebrate a family member, Nathaniel Scott, on his ninetieth birthday. A more recent creation was a poem about my cousin, Wilsie Calhoun, whose life's purpose is to serve as our family historian.

I have a collection of poems, some dating back to the 1980s, in their original form. I hired someone to format them with a graphic or background. As the designer finished each one, my heart beamed with joy. She seemed to understand my perspective at the time of writing, yet transformed them into her unique interpretation, as poetry should be. I envisioned them as pages in an anthology, a basal reader, or published as *My Book of Poems II* by Jeri D. Dokes. The first signed copy reserved for my brother.

Of all my writing, my greatest joy and accomplishment has been my self-published book, *Dear Aunt Daisy, I'm Telling You the Truth.* The poem turned children's picture book tells a quaint story of the time my siblings and I spent the summer on our Uncle Robert and Aunt Daisy's farm. Our parents taught us to work together and follow the rules. Theirs were no different. The message serves as a reflection of my life; however, adults enjoy sharing it with their children and grandchildren as an example of their values and principles. The book includes activity pages to engage readers, apply comprehension strategies, and build vocabulary. Since the 2018 original publishing, I created a practice test that aligns with Ohio's Common Core State Standards. I used state test questioning techniques to give students an opportunity to master the controversial testing method. My goal is to help them convert daily learning into ongoing success.

The success I have experienced in writing probably originated from the early support and motivation that I received from my parents. My siblings, the "other" Jacksons, and I, produce hits that keep us at the top of the charts by encouraging one another. Formal training and experience in journalism and news writing, along with my career as an English teacher, contributed to my accomplishments.

Many writers with a profound ability in storytelling are successful by taking a couple classes to organize their writing into factual accounts (non-fiction) or creative narration (fiction). Others have a basic understanding of writing learned in grade school. Then, there are those who write from the heart and seek an editor to revise their work.

Regardless of where you are on the writing spectrum, I encourage you to set your sights on your goals...your destiny. As with any learning process, the sooner you start, the better.

My motto for anyone who wants to write and publish is you can do it! That's my guiding principle for encouraging students, those who inquire about my writing journey, and as a reminder to myself when doubt creeps in. Every writer needs editing, revision, and sometimes elaboration. Success in writing requires two things: a desire to reach your writing goal and an investment of time. Even with all my experience, it wasn't until I set a goal to write and publish my book, and invest the time to see it to completion, that I held the official title of author. I did it, you can do it, too!

For as long as I can remember, Mom reminded us to do our best. She reinforced her words by leading by example. She wanted to go to college, but did not have the means. In her later years, she took writing classes at Sinclair Community College. She created a thoughtful poem titled what else? *Destiny*.

A seasoned educator with twenty-five years in the classroom and five years as an instructional coach, Jeri D. Dokes is passionate about developing children into leaders. She uses her love for short stories and poetry as a teaching tool. In her Homework Cafe Writing Camp sessions, she instills ownership in learning, and pride in accomplishment while teaching the power of narrative and creative writing. The process initiates a logical progression of skills that invite the writer to draft stories and poetry creating budding authors. An advocate for healthy family relationships, Dokes incorporated her childhood experiences on a farm where she learned responsibility, work ethic, and respect for elders to create her children's picture book, *Dear Aunt Daisy, I'm Telling You the Truth.*

Connect with Jeri
Amazon.com/author/jeriddokes
Facebook.com/Jeri.Dokes
LinkedIn.com/in/jeri-d-dokes-m-ed-a0326b75

Jeri's Favorite Resource
SelfPublishingAdvisor.com. In addition to other reference books on publishing, this site is a great place to find the most up-to-date information and changes in the world of indie book publishing.

Crafting Compelling Stories that Tug at the Hearts of Your Readers

Bridget Flaherty

Growing up, every Sunday after church, we visited my great-grandmother, my father's mother's mother, Lavina Wolfe. She was born in 1889 on a farm in Ohio with no running water and no electricity. She lived through both World Wars, The Great Depression, the advent of radio and telephone, the invention of the automobile, and the interstate highway system. She watched Kennedy get shot on television. She remembered the shock of Pearl Harbor and the impact of the Civil Rights Movement. She watched a man step on the moon. My beloved great-grandmother was 87 when I was born, and I was 13 when she died.

On those Sunday drives to Grandma's house, my father often reminded us that we did not know how much time we had left with her. He said, "Remember to make the most of today because today might be our last day with her. We just don't know. Grandma is really old."

Entertained with imaginary play, I opened the old, chipped, creaky metal kitchen cabinets. I took out the tin and copper cups and bowls. They were different from the cups and bowls we had at home. Grandma's dishes were light, and they didn't break when I hit them against one another to make noise. I pretended to make cakes and tea. I took the bowls full of imagination over to my grandmother, who always sat at the head of the kitchen table. She was close enough to open the refrigerator without leaving her chair, while talking to my parents and the other adults who visited. Regardless of what was going on at the table, when I presented my tea and cakes, my grandmother stopped and pretended to sip the tea and eat the cake. She picked me up, sat me on her lap, and gave me kisses.

As I got older, I noticed that sometimes, depending on what I brought to the table, she set down the item and told a story to the adults about whatever it was.

I gathered things around the house that I didn't know what they were, especially if they seemed really old, and I brought them to her. "Grandma, what's this?"

One time there was a heavy metal thing with a handle next to the fireplace in the kitchen. I wanted to know what it was, so I picked it up, struggling with its weight, and I brought it to her. It was so heavy I couldn't lift it to the table. Standing there, holding this black metal block with two hands, I said, "Grandma, what is this?"

Gently, she said, "Put it on the floor, dear."

I did.

"Do you know how your mom irons your dad's shirts?"

"Yes."

"Why do you think it's called an iron?"

"I don't know."

"Well, that is why," pointing to the heavy metal block on the floor. "That is an iron. It is made out of iron. Before electricity, if you wanted to press your shirt or a tablecloth, you put that iron in the fire. Once it got really hot, you took it out of the fire and put it on a stand." She pointed to the stand next to the fireplace. "You let it cool down a little, and then used it to press shirts, tablecloths, or your hair." She explained that if you wanted to straighten your hair, you spread out your hair on the ironing board and use the iron to press it.

She turned to the table of adults and told them a story about the time her younger sister had a date and wanted to straighten her hair. They prepped the iron in the fire, took it out to cool, but her sister was in a hurry and didn't want to wait. Her date was on his way! My grandmother warned her sister, but her sister insisted. As soon as the iron touched her sister's hair, they smelled it burning. The horrid smell filled the house. They had to cut her sister's hair before her date arrived.

"I don't think that my sister ever forgave me for singeing her hair even after she had been married to that man for forty years."

Everyone at the table laughed.

From that story on, every time we visited my grandmother, I pulled over a stepstool chair high enough for me to sit at the kitchen table next to her. Instead of playing on the floor with my siblings, I listened to the stories she shared.

One particular story I asked my grandmother to tell me over and over again like it was my favorite bedtime story. Actually, it was my absolute favorite.

Every year, she and her nine siblings helped her father harvest food from their farm and put it into a horse-drawn wagon. Her father and uncle took it to market. One year, the harvest was exceptionally fruitful. They made lots of money selling what they had grown. Her father and uncle were excited about the amount of money they had made and wanted to celebrate. They saw a man selling exotic fruit from South America, so they decided to buy this fruit that they had never heard of before. The salesman raved about how sweet the fruit was and how far he had come to bring it to them. This exotic fruit cost five cents.

My grandmother leaned down toward me. "Now remember, five cents back then could buy you two Hershey bars the size of your head." She held up her hands to both sides of her head to show the size of the chocolate bar. "Two bananas for ten cents was a lot of money, but they were excited to eat those sweet treats from a faraway place because this was a celebration!"

As soon as they took a bite of their bananas, they spit them out, complaining that they were tough, bitter, and barely edible. They wondered how anyone could ever eat these things. They were angry. They felt like they had been swindled into buying an inedible fruit from a snake oil salesman. They threw the bananas in the trash and came home with the story.

My grandmother leaned in close to me and quietly asked, "Why do you think that is?"

"I don't know," drawing out my words, faking innocence so that she could deliver the punchline.

"Because no one told them that they had to peel the bananas!"

I laughed every single time.

My siblings and cousins told that story after Lavina Wolfe passed on at the age of 100 years young. I told the story to my children. When my grandson was three years old, my daughter sent me a video telling the banana story to him, Lavina Wolfe's great-great-great-grandson. He laughed a big belly laugh at the punchline, just like I had more than forty years earlier.

That is the power of a personal story. It lives on in the hearts and minds of your listeners and readers long after you're gone.

As a story coach, I often hear people say things like, "I don't have any stories." Or "No one wants to hear my stories." This could not be further from the truth.

No way could my grandmother have foreseen the impact of her story on the generations that came after her or how storytelling would become my passion and profession. Instead, she simply shared her life with her grandchildren.

Your life, story, experiences, passions, knowledge, and expertise are essential and valuable. They can also be contagious and memorable.

Marketing your book will often involve personal appearances, speaking engagements, book signings, interviews, and panel discussions. Sharing stories is the most powerful way to connect your audience to you and your book because our brains are wired for stories. Humans have been telling stories longer than we have been creating art on cave walls. Stories were how we passed information from one generation to the next before the written word. Stories captivate our minds and sink into our memories in ways that other forms of information do not.

So, how do you craft your personal story? First, focus on a moment that conveys an idea or represents a value you want to share with the audience. This moment was impactful for you in some way. It changed you, or it provides context for the event. For example, you may tell a story about the first time you saw your book on a shelf in a bookstore or about the moment you decided that you were going to write a book. You may choose to tell a story about your childhood or a mentor who gave you the courage to try something new.

Here are a few ways to find your story:

Focus on the Theme

If you have been given a theme for a presentation or a specific message that you want to convey, write the theme at the top of a piece of paper.

Next, rapidly list any people, places, or things that come to mind when you think of that theme. For example, if the speech is about innovation, list all of the technology, inventions, processes, people, companies, business conferences, cities, etc. that come to mind. Write this list quickly and keep writing until the nouns are coming more slowly or a memory hits you, and you know that it is the one.

Read through the list and identify a memory for each word that you wrote. Then, write a few things about the memory to help you remember what story (or stories) goes with that word.

Continue through the list until you have a couple of stories to tell. To choose a story, consider the following:

- How strongly the story supports the theme or message you want to convey.
- How well you remember the details.
- How comfortable you are with sharing the story.
- Does it match the audience?
- Does it conjure emotion?

Narrow your choices to one. Circle it. You have identified a story!

What Happened First?

Think about the first time you did something or the first time something happened. These firsts may be memorable moments, or they might help you to think of other times that are worth sharing. The story that comes to mind may not be the first time, but a memorable one. Follow where your memory takes you! These firsts are designed to jog your memory and help you identify a story, even if it wasn't the first.

First job	First client
First sale	First publication
First child	First kiss
First love	First day on the job
First interview	First trip
First car	First date
First big success	First big mistake

Jot notes for any of these firsts that resonate with you. If another memory comes to mind, follow the memory trail, and make notes that will help you remember the story. Read through your notes, pick one memory that jumps out at you, and circle it. You have a story!

<u>Answer the Question with a Story</u>

Another way to find a story is to answer prompts. Think about common questions from readers, customers, or colleagues. What story can you use to answer those questions?

Using the prompts below or questions you regularly receive, follow the memory trail. Allow your mind to wander into meaningful memories that make good stories.

- Tell me about a time you found a solution to a difficult problem.
- Tell me about a time you had to be resourceful.

- Tell me about a terrible day.
- Tell me about your best day.
- Tell me about a time you turned an angry customer into a loyal one.
- Tell me about the mentor who made you believe in yourself.
- Tell me an embarrassing moment that changed you.
- What is the hardest thing you have done in your professional or personal life?
- What is your proudest moment?
- Tell me about the time everything changed.
- Tell me a story about your favorite teacher or coach.
- Tell me about a time someone said that you couldn't do something, and you proved them wrong.

Make note of moments that jump out to you as you read these questions. Then, pick one that is meaningful and craft the story.

<u>The Story Arc</u>
A story has a beginning, a middle, and an end and focuses on one particular moment in time. For example, it zooms in on the moment where a conflict is resolved, a problem overcame, a question answered, or a lesson learned. The beginning gives the listener context for the moment. The middle focuses on what happened in the moment. The end conveys the impact by telling the listener how things

are after the moment has passed. To further explain the story arc, I use this image when conducting the LORE workshop for storytellers.

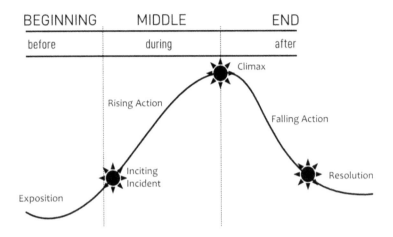

The timeline is the path of what happened or series of events. You may choose to start with the climax and work backwards, covering the middle before explaining the beginning for dramatic effect. However, the story must still contain all three elements. Therefore, if you begin with the climax, you must return to the beginning so that the reader understands the context.

The beginning, or the exposition, sets up the reader/listener by explaining the context before the main part of the story happened. It explains what you were like, what the world was like, what was normal. The beginning also introduces the characters and gives the reader the background. The beginning sets the stage for what happens, so the readers know what they need to know to understand the story.

The middle is the meat of the story. It is what happened. Starting with an inciting incident, something that sets the story in motion, followed by the rising action, the middle builds to the story's climax, the moment that your readers are waiting for.

The middle explains what you did, how you felt, what was at stake, what you wanted to happen, and what actually happened. It explains the decisions, the conflict, the agony, and the laughter. The middle is where you explain to your readers what happened and why.

The story reaches the tipping point at the climax, when tensions are at their highest, and the most exciting or important actions occur. This is the moment that changed you or the characters in the story. This is the point after which it was not the same.

The end of the story wraps up the middle for your readers by providing a resolution. It explains the story's impact, how you or the world are different, what you learned, how you were changed, and why it matters. The end leaves the readers feeling the way you want them to feel: outraged, inspired, calm, emotional, called to action, confused, etc.

Five Essential Components to Craft Your Story

The five essential components to crafting a personal story are theme, characters, descriptions, dialogue, and tone or voice. Let's explore these components and how to incorporate them into your story.

What is the message behind your story?

The theme is the reason you are telling your story. It keeps your story in bounds, like guardrails, providing clarity. The theme provides focus and a reference point when deciding what aspects belong and what should be cut.

When deciding your theme, ask yourself: What do you want your readers to feel or do? What actions do you want them to take after reading/hearing your story? For example, do you want them to buy something from you? Do you want them to donate money to a non-profit? Do you want to inspire them to work more collaboratively or with more dedication? Do you want them to believe in a mission? Do you want them to wonder about their purpose? Do you want them to ask more questions? Do you want them to believe in something?

The theme gives your story context. The same series of events—what happened—can be told in different ways depending on your theme. What details you share, what emotions you convey, and how you end the story help to leave readers/listeners with a message to which they can connect.

Deciding why you are sharing the story and what you want your readers/listeners to feel and remember is essential for crafting your story. For example, in choosing to share about my grandmother's stories and how influential they were, the story's theme, "the power of stories," is understood without being stated. By the end of my story, you understand how my grandmother inspired my love of stories and how contagious stories are passed from one person to another.

Who is in the story?
Every story needs identifiable characters. Without characters, it isn't a story. Characters give us someone to care about, someone to root for, someone to connect with. Once you have identified your characters, describe them. Choose which characteristics to include based on what you want your readers/listeners to envision in their minds. Suppose you describe a character's attitude instead of physical appearance. In that case, your audience will relate the character to someone similar in their minds. For example, if you focus on how a bully made you feel and not how they looked, the reader/listener will imagine a bully from their life. However, if you describe a specific person in your life, like a mentor, describing what he or she looked like might help your audience imagine them specifically.

In most stories, you are the primary character, and the story is told from your point of view. Something happened to you, you witnessed something happening to someone, or you heard about something that happened.

First-person narratives, things that happened to you, connect you to the reader because you express how you felt, what you saw, where you were, and how you were affected. It is your real experience of the events. So you, as the main character, are the go-to for real-life storytelling.

Because you are the main character, it is essential to understand yourself as a character and describe yourself with the same level of detail as other characters. So often, we focus on the other characters forgetting that we are an important part of the story.

Relatable, imaginable characters are vital to a great story. Here are a few things to consider when developing your characters:

- Physical characteristics: What does he/she/they look like? Think about eye color, hair color, physical build, age, etc.
- Clothing and accessories: Describe what s/he might have worn. Think about style and time frame. What car did they drive? What were they carrying? Use these details to paint a picture of who they were/are based on what they wear, drive, or carry.
- Possessions that represent who they are: List a few things that the character owned or used that represent them. For example, grandma's teakettle or your coach's whistle. Describe the object and why it reminds you of that person.
- Likes, dislikes, fears, aspirations: Tell us what motivates the character. What did s/he fear at the time? Or what were they seeking?
- Actions, passions, training, experience: Similarly, tell us about the character's

qualifications, their past, and where they were going.

- Mannerisms: Tell us about repeated patterns or interesting quirks your character had. Maybe they repeated a phrase or always entered a room a specific way.
- History between characters: Tell us about your history with the character or the history between two characters. If you are the character, tell us how you are different now than you were then.
- How do you feel about the character? How do other characters feel about the character? What emotional response do you have when you think about this character?

In describing my great-grandmother, I told you her age, how she grew up, and how I felt when she lifted me onto her lap. These descriptions bring her to life, encouraging the reader to picture an older woman sitting at a kitchen table surrounded by children and adults. Likewise, developing your characters, including yourself, helps to endear listeners to you and the other people in your story.

Descriptions: Emotions and the Scene
Descriptions bring a story to life. They conjure a picture in the listener's mind. There are two critical parts of story descriptions.

Emotions: Tell us how you felt. The most critical descriptions to include in your story are your feelings and reactions. Take time to describe how you felt about what was happening in the story. Readers will connect to the emotions even if they have not experienced similar events. For example, they may not have ever lost a job, but they understand fear, disappointment, embarrassment, and anger.

Scene: Allow the reader/listener to join you on the trip down memory lane. Describe specific details to create imagery that brings the moment to life. Describing the color of the sky and the weather, along with what the characters wore, paints a picture for your audience.

When describing a scene, keep your audience in mind. Make sure that they can relate to the descriptions and imagine the scene. Be sure to explain industry-specific terms and acronyms when appropriate. Be aware of time-specific references that might not be understood by people who are not in your age bracket. A few words to explain a world event, popular song, or lack of cell phones will keep them with you. Any time someone is wondering about something you wrote or said, they aren't engaged. Clear, concise, and specific descriptions take the reader/listener on a journey with you so that they don't fall behind.

Details matter! For example, in my story, the kitchen descriptions, the iron, the chair that I sat on are small details that bring the scene to life. The reader/listener is in the room with me. Similarly, describing how she gave me kisses and attention hints at how I felt about the family matriarch. How I responded to her story, laughing at the punchline, is childlike and innocent.

What do the characters say to one another?

We often use dialogue to describe what happened when sharing a story with a friend or co-worker. For example, you might say something like: "He said, 'Blah blah.' I just couldn't believe it. So, I told him, 'Blah blah blah.' Do you want to know what he said next?"

Dialogue advances the story, develops the characters, and brings a dynamic element to the story. Although a story does not require dialogue, it helps to provide realism, information, and context in an entertaining way.

The back-and-forth conversation between the child version of me and my grandmother creates a picture in the reader/listener's mind. They are taken into the moment as if witnessing the conversation happening in front of them. The characters are alive, talking to one another.

Tone or Voice

Everyone has a natural voice, a particular way of speaking. Think about the stories that you tend to tell repeatedly and the tone you use.

Voice and tone reflect your attitude about the subject and the readers. It conveys how you feel about the story. Although each story will have its own tone, knowing your personal way of speaking will define how you craft your story so that the authentic you comes through to your audience.

To find your voice, recall the last three conversations you had where you shared something about your life. What did you talk about? Did your listeners laugh? Did they cry? Were they surprised? Were you frustrated or irritated? Is there a common tone to these conversations? How would you describe your tone in each conversation?

With this information, craft your story using your natural way of speaking. For example, my natural voice is emotional, focusing on stories that bring tears to my eyes. Typically, they are nostalgic and heartwarming. However, the story about my great-grandmother is infused with a bit of humor. Therefore, knowing my usual way of speaking is important but not restrictive.

Taking time to craft your personal story is a powerful way to engage an audience or launch a marketing campaign. Pick one meaningful moment. Outline the beginning, middle, and end, using the five essential components and you will craft a compelling story.

Next time you are invited to a speaking engagement or a book signing, start with a powerful story. Engage your audience with an emotional, vulnerable, memorable story from your life. As they remember the story, they will remember the storyteller.

Following a successful career in information technology, business process improvement, and organizational change management, Bridget Flaherty became a master storyteller. Odd transition? Yes. The combination of experiences uniquely qualified her to teach storytelling for business. The first time Bridget stood on stage to tell a story; she won the competition. She was hooked. She traveled to share stories and soon recognized that captivating stories can influence business success. Bridget developed a curriculum for business professionals by marrying more than fifteen years of experience in business leadership with her passion for storytelling. She facilitates storytelling workshops, small group sessions, and one-on-one coaching for individuals who want to improve presentation skills, increase sales, gather customer testimonials, and change company culture.

Connect with Bridget
LoreStorytelling.com
Facebook.com/StorytellingLore
LinkedIn.com/company/Lore-Storytelling
Instagram.com/LoreStorytelling
Twitter.com/LoreCulture

Bridget's Favorite Resource
TheMoth.org promotes the art and craft of storytelling while providing resources and training on how to make your story more engaging.

Writing Christian Devotionals from the H.E.A.R.T.

Dr. Cheri Westmoreland

The Greek word—kardia—appears over one thousand times in the Bible as heart. It is the most common anthropological term in Scripture[3]. Biblical scholars said that the heart is the seat of life or strength. The mind, soul, spirit, emotional nature, and understanding are connected to the heart. In the Aramaic culture, the heart is the organ with the ability to reason, question, meditate, and think. As writers with a passion for sharing God's Word, the heart is the central or innermost guide in the writing process. My writing integrates passion for Christ and an acronym for heart as the framework to bring clarity to devotional messages.

Christian devotionals are short pieces of biblical inspiration. Many devotionals draw upon a three-step format focused on Scripture. This illustration speaks to the reader and presents a simple, applicable truth. I started writing devotionals with this useful format.

Prayer provides guidance, direction, and focus for influencing the world, so I sought God for what He wanted me to say. A support team of prayer

---

[3] Easton, George Matthew, *Baker's Illustrated Bible Dictionary*, Baker Book House, 1981.

warriors encouraged, interceded, and mentored me while writing the messages of inspiration. This foundation of prayer strengthens, builds, and sustains the heart to write devotionals.

In collaboration with Crystal Huie Arnold, *Prayers Go Up: The Prophetic Artist Devotional Journal* was created. This devotional is an experience with prophetic artwork, Scripture, reflective thought, and prayer. Note pages are provided for readers to reflect, seek God for personal revelation, and create a life application.

This Scripture is the guiding principle for my writing:

> *Write down the revelation and make it plain*
> *on tablets so that a herald may run with it.*
> —Habakkuk 2:2

This Scripture speaks to my focus on writing devotionals:

> *For where your treasure is, there your heart*
> *will be also.*
> —Matthew 6:21

The words are the treasures coming from the heart of God, which is revealed to me through prayer and fasting. The call to write is to share the gospel of Jesus Christ and inspire people to seek godly wisdom and truth. As I reflected on my writing journey with *Prayers Go Up*, I approached it from the H.E.A.R.T:

- H - Handle your God-given topic with prayer.
- E – Enter into prayer for Scriptures as the anchor for the devotional.
- A – Ask reflection questions to personalize the reader's experience.
- R – Review devotional topics, Scriptures, and reflection questions for consistency and clarity.
- T – inTimacy with God

Handle with Prayer

For several years, I wrote about faith and prayer. I embraced and appreciated my God-given topic to empower and do kingdom work. My first experience working with prayer was as the prayer coordinator for the Emmaus Community in Northern Kentucky. I encouraged members to be part of the three-day prayer vigil for the semi-annual Emmaus Walk. My role was minor, but it exposed me to prayer and its transformative influence.

A committee of thirty women was charged to pray for the needs of specific programs and events. To coordinate the group effort, I developed a prayer calendar to share daily devotionals. Many women were encouraged and developed a stronger, consistent prayer life. Transitioning the daily devotionals to a thirty-day devotional journal was easy.

Prayers Go Up: The Prophetic Artist is a collection of twenty-one illustrations, including nine abstract art pieces that appear to be people praying in different positions. The artwork was a creative step to express my thoughts and God's insights while providing an interactive element for readers. After praying about the art, it was revealed to me to use the fruit of the Spirit to identify the nine poses. Prayers were developed encouraging readers to seek God on how to incorporate each fruit of the Spirit into their daily lives.

Enter into Prayer

Praying for Scriptures to anchor the devotional is essential. Spending time with God opens your heart and mind to see His fullness. You can start by developing a prayer calendar by topic or subject area. My prayer calendars were created for the forty days before Easter and thirty days before a women's ministry event. We prayed for leadership, members, vision, and God's direction for committee members.

Since my devotional included original artwork, I prayed for Scriptures that aligned with the images and how to convey the meaning. Six art pieces included women with corresponding titles Meditative, Steadfast, Noble, Matrix, Concerned, and Thoughtful. These descriptions led me to character-building Scriptures. A Bible concordance was another tool I used to find Scriptures that illustrated the truth God wanted revealed for the art.

Six landscape pieces revealed more about His character as Creator using bodies of water, flourishing plants, and starry skies. The companion

Scriptures aligned with the beauty of all created things.

Ask Reflection Questions

Reflection questions help create an interactive and transformative experience as readers apply the truth of God to their lives. These open-ended questions are crafted with intention by thinking about the responses you desire for your readers.

Because the purpose is for readers to assess how a concept influenced them, create questions specific to each devotional topic or use these common questions:

- What surprised you in this devotional?
- What is the most important thing you learned?
- How can you implement what you learned?

My devotionals include the following questions:

- How much time are you spending with the Lord each day?
- What talents, skills, or abilities has God given you for ministry?
- What worry or concern do you need to give to God?

In Christian devotionals, reflective writing engages deeper understanding and continuous learning. The goal of reflection is spiritual growth and making conscientious decisions in line with godly principles. It can empower writers and readers to

> *Do your best to present yourself to God as one approved, a worker who does not need to be ashamed and who correctly handles the Word of truth.*
> —2 Timothy 2:15

Review

Review the devotional topic, Scriptures, and reflection questions to clarify the message of the devotion. At times, you may need more illustrations or stories to help the reader understand the simple truth. An example of reviewing for clarity includes categorizing the devotions to see if the message is consistent. For example, in *Prayers Go Up*, art pieces represent praying positions, women of prayer, and landscaped environments conducive for prayer.

Another strategy I use to clarify the message is concluding the devotional with a prayer. Prayer is communication with God to praise Him, request help, and seek forgiveness. Prayers can be spoken, silent, or sung.

Writing prayers tapped into the area of ministry that I am passionate to serve. The prayers conveyed love and spiritual growth to become a workman approved by Him. I wrote prayers to thank God for the devotional's message. I asked for help to apply the truth of the message to my life and my readers' lives.

Write prayers to communicate with a sincere heart. Begin by thanking God for all He has done through the message. Make it a personal letter that meets the needs and concerns for growth and development in Christ Jesus. End your written prayers with the purest form of closure, "Amen," which means "so be it."

Genuine prayers come from the heart. If you are unfamiliar with writing prayers, keep a journal of your daily prayers. From those encounters with God, rivers of living water will flow. You will write prayers that help reveal the mysteries of God. Open your heart to receive from Him and give to others.

InTimacy with God

I cherish this phase most in my writing journey. I schedule time to get away, write, and spend quality time with Him. I dedicate my thoughts to focus on what God says to me. I write His words for revelation knowledge. This sweet moment is perfect for incorporating H.E.A.R.T. principles and drawing upon God's interpretation of the writing.

Finding the right place and time to commune with the Lord is critical. Establish a private, cozy space. It may be a day when you're home alone, a weekend get-away at a hotel, or a weeklong retreat without distractions from the outside world. Start creating intimacy with God by implementing any of these suggestions.

Writing from the heart brings you closer to the Lord while providing your readers with an example of how He desires them to draw near to Him. Prepare the ground for your readers to

> *Seek the Lord while He may be found; call*
> *on Him while He is near.*
> —Isaiah 55:6

Let your words flow from the H.E.A.R.T. and help connect your readers to the wonders of the Lord Jesus Christ.

Dr. Cheri Westmoreland is founder of Spirit Excel, LLC which energizes, empowers, and elevates faith and community-based organizations to enhance professional excellence. Dr. Cheri has worked in higher education and community-based agencies for over thirty years. Through pain and disappointment, she journaled to the Lord, which helped heal her heartache and inspired her to share her transformation with others. She chronicled her faith walk and healing work in three anthologies: *Conversations on Faith, Prayers Go Up: Prophetic Art Devotional Journal,* and *Twelve Women: Inspirational Journeys of Faith, Hope, and Love.*

Connect with Dr. Cheri
SpiritExcel.org
Facebook.com/cheri.westmoreland.35
Linkedin.com/in/Dr-Cheri-Westmoreland-19989b19

Dr. Cheri's Favorite Resource
FlourishWritersAcademy.com is designed as a yearlong journey to set goals, implement a plan, and adjust as progress is achieved. This community provides resources and support for Christian writers who desire long-term growth and development.

Finding Your Writing Voice after Corporate Laryngitis

Dr. Velma Bagby

In a corporate environment, your writing voice is quieted. Corporate laryngitis. You cannot add your opinion in an official capacity, written or verbal.

I worked for thirty-eight years as a state employee. I oversaw programs and services at local employment centers comprised of more than 100 staff and managers. Managing budgets, premises, personnel, and processes by applying a host of analytical tools was essential. With my voice silenced, they groomed me to be a representative of the state government. I carried their brand and messaging. Formal communication was concise, uniform phrases that had been designed and filtered through the legal department. Communications with my teams, partners, and customers were consistent with the state's policy and messaging. Written and verbal communications did not reflect my voice, opinion, or creativity.

I was active in church ministry. Although a nonprofit organization, the ministry also represented a corporate voice. I taught Sunday school, facilitated classes for women, and served as an instructor of theology classes. Church had its brand and messaging.

Imagine how difficult it was for me to find my writing voice since I had not used it in almost four decades. Upon retirement, I was ready to write my first book. My dilemma: How do I transition from a corporate voice to my own?

It is time to set aside what you learned in corporate. The following tips helped me rediscover my writing voice and they will simplify your transition.

A Writing Voice

While in corporate, your writing reflects the company brand, messaging, and opinion. Finding your voice involves knowing your brand, your genre, and your message for the intended audience. Your writing voice reflects your creative style in character development, how you structure phrases, the plot, and story. Your writing voice becomes how readers identify you. It's one aspect of what they like about you as an author.

Once you discover your writing voice, your creativity is no longer silenced. Your messaging is no longer one-size-fits-all because you can think outside of the box. At that moment, you no longer suffer from corporate laryngitis. Your audience hears what you have to say how you want to say it. Congratulations! You found your writing voice.

The Corporate World Uses a One-Size-Fits-All Method to Writing

The state government trained staff to use an official template for written communications; the one-size-fits-all method of writing. In creative writing, no such method exists. You are free to use any method including the Chapter Outline Method, Snowflake Method, and more. It is important that you find the method that works for you.

I struggled to write my book using the traditional method because my style is less organized. I assumed my struggle was personal, until an author friend suggested the Chapter Outline Method. My first attempt applying this method was frustrating. I shredded my sample. I hated it! I assumed the issue was with me and my writing, until I discovered something unique about my style.

My writing method was not wrong, it was different. I remember the day I experienced my aha moment. I conducted a Google search to explore other methods. So many results, but the popular ones were the Snowflake Method, Outline Method, Post-it Notes, and 30-Day Method. The method that set my writing free and liberated me to be comfortable with my writing style was the Jigsaw Method. "Free at last!"

With the Jigsaw Method, you do not write from beginning to end. Writing is based on the section of the story you are most excited about versus structured, regimented order. This describes my method! I can address a section or skip to the back of the book. I can return to a piece I worked on earlier. As my writing unfolds, I take the pieces I have written and put them together, much like assembling jigsaw puzzle pieces. This method allows free-flowing creativity. Remember to accept who you are as a writer and you can do this, too. No method is right or wrong, but there is a method that works best for you.

Corporate Uses Empty Adverbs, Not Dialogue

Writing action and dialogue may prove difficult in the beginning because corporate writing has adverb-itis, an overuse of empty adverbs. This device makes writing quick without requiring explanation or backstory. However, in creative writing, it is important to eliminate pairing a verb with an empty—or weak—adverb. At times, adverbs are appropriate, but do not overuse them.

Here are examples of adverb-*itis* and how to correct them:

> He talked rapidly versus Words exited his mouth at a rapid rate of speed
> She advanced quickly versus She wasted little time lunging toward her

As a visual learner, I enjoy reading books with great descriptions and imagery. On the contrary, I do not enjoy books with pages of dialogue in which every sentence begins with "he said," "she said," or "they said."

For example,

> "Hi," said John.
> Katie said, "How are you doing?"
> John said, "Pretty good."
> Katie said...aggravating!

Create your own tips or find online tip sheets that will help you avoid dialogue mistakes. I found several, but my favorite is *280 Different Ways to Say Said* (see *Your Bestseller Resources* on page 141). Look for tips on how to structure dialogue and infuse action referred to as indirect dialogue.

Here is the revised dialogue example:

> John revved the engine of his new Porsche hoping to get Katie's attention. He pulled down his sunglasses, peered over the top of the frames. "Hi."
> Embarrassed, she couldn't hide her reddened cheeks. Without looking at him, she said, "How are you doing?"

Corporate Writing Ignores the Five Senses

Corporate writing gets straight to the point. It's clean and precise. As with other communications, protocol required the legal screening process to ensure the verbiage maintained the brand. It was not designed to be descriptive, and sensory writing was not the focus.

In creative writing, every author needs to master tapping into the five senses for powerful storytelling. Using sensory writing to describe characters, scenes, and events pulls readers into your story. You want to build a picture in your readers' minds to keep them engaged and wanting more.

I used *Cheat Sheets for Writing Body Language* (see *Resources to Write Your Bestseller*) to translate emotions (parenthesis) into <u>written body language</u>:

> He <u>clasped his hands behind his body, bit his bottom lip, and kicked at imaginary rocks</u>. (hiding his feelings)
> With her <u>shoulders slumped</u>, she <u>looked down and away</u>. (shame)

You can find a host of tip sheets online to build your writing arsenal. I organize mine in a folder entitled "Writing Helps." The more you read, learn, and practice, the less you will reference your tip sheets.

Corporate Uses the Tell-Don't-Show Rule

The golden rule of creative writing opposes this corporate rule. Show-don't-tell is one of the biggest adjustments when moving from corporate writing to finding your voice. Corporate writing is straightforward, whereas creative writing gives details to draw readers into a character, experience, or scene. Use the five senses to show your audience what is happening to evoke emotions, feelings, and responses to your message.

The show-don't-tell rule reinforces a creative writing process that is more descriptive, expressive, and emotional. Here is an example of <u>written body language</u> to show versus tell:

Tell: Sam was angry.
Show**:** Sam <u>grit his teeth.</u> With an <u>intense glare</u> and his <u>body shaking</u>, he <u>slammed his fists</u> on the table.

Instead of telling readers how a character feels, show them. Anger, happiness, and love look different on everyone. Master this rule by researching examples to restore your voice from corporate laryngitis.

Invest in a Writing Tool to Help You Transition from Corporate Writing

I used a great writing tool to help me turn off that corporate voice by highlighting issues like tell-don't-show. With practice, I transformed my writing.

My go-to tool is <u>ProWritingAid.com</u>. I prefer this tool because it helps identify corporate-style writing, provides rephrased options, and checks grammar. Not only did it serve as a training tool, it reminded me when I retreated to corporate writing. ProWritingAid identified other corporate writing habits:

- Beginning too many sentences with the same word
- Too many duplicate or overused words in the same paragraph
- Excessive use of adverbs
- Use of past tense, a corporate habit, when present tense is required.
- All narrative, which is instructional and telling. The dialogue checker helps shift your writing to showing, which is critical for creative writing.

Write, and Trust the Experts

Practice is the road to refining your writing skills. It took me six years to finish my first book, which included multiple versions and revisions. Had I consulted with an expert early in the process, I could have addressed my challenges and discovered my voice sooner. You cannot improve something you have not done. But do not write alone!

Connect with an expert or mentor. Authors tend to not set aside money for guidance, but I believe in budgeting for expert help. Since an expert cannot help you with a blank sheet of paper, begin your journey. Get started. Write!

Write, and Learn to "Beta"

A beta reader provides feedback based on what your average reader loves to read. They identify gaps in your details, inconsistencies, and more. They serve as representatives of your target audience and do not replace professional editors.

When writing my eBook, *My 70s Love Story*, about how my husband and I met, I received great recommendations from my beta group. One beta reader's suggestion caught my attention because she spotlighted some of my corporate habits. She asked me to add more dialogue and details between characters. She referenced where I wrote about our first date, but I did not provide any specific details. She asked:

- What kind of car was he driving?
- What did he wear?
- What cologne did he wear?
- What songs played on the radio?
- What did I wear?
- What did we discuss while riding?
- Where did we go or what did we do?

You can see how corporate writing is lazy writing. It is quick and provides no details other than excessive adverbs. Thanks to my beta readers who exposed my corporate voice. Be careful. Practice will help you avoid reverting back to old habits.

Learning is a Lifelong Process...Read

The more you read, the better you'll write. Read books to help your transition and continuous growth. You'll learn different writing styles, literary devices, and tips to hone your craft.

Read books by authors in the genre you like. Choose those who tell a story similar to the style you want to develop. If you start with authors who are twenty years into their career, you may be intimidated. Consider studying the works of authors closer to your starting point. For best results and to set a benchmark for excellence, follow authors with high ratings on Amazon. As your writing improves, advance to the next level.

Read books that provide writing guidelines. Learn the language of writing a book: point of view (POV), first, second, or third person, plot, character development, dialogue, chapter hooks, narrative, and more. Marketing elements like synopses, taglines, and keywords are imperative to your success.

Read your work out loud, alone, and with a group. Some versions of Microsoft Word have an audible feature. You can listen to your story to catch mistakes and identify areas for rewrites.

Clear your throat!

As CEO of Adoni Publishing, Dr. Velma has penned books in multiple genres. Dr. Velma co-authored and published a children's book with her six-year-old granddaughter. *The Little Letter k* is a story of alphabet characters with human personalities. The book won the 2020 Story Monsters Approved Book Award. She helps Christians experience fulfilling, romantic relationships referencing her 47-year marriage and 38-year career with the State of California. She serves single women to recognize their worth, counsels couples considering marriage, and salvages spouses from divorce. She offers tips on dating, relationships, and marriage on her weekly Facebook Lives.

Connect with Dr. Velma
DrVelma.com
Amazon.com/author/drvelmabagby
Facebook.com/DrVelmaB
Linkedin.com/in/dr-velma-bagby-85b476125
Instagram.com/DrVelmaBagby_author
Twitter.com/BagbyVelma

Dr. Velma's Favorite Resource
After publishing my first book through a hybrid company, I was determined to learn as much as I could. Kindlepreneur.com is full of free guides and resources that propelled me to become an independent author.

_____

_____

_____

_____

_____

_____

_____

_____

_____

_____

_____

_____

_____

_____

_____

_____

_____

_____

_____

5 Writing Tips for Self-Care & Success

Nelson O. O. Zounlome, Ph.D.

Having attended a predominantly White institution for undergraduate and graduate school, I experienced discrimination, gendered racism, and being viewed as less qualified than my White peers. With my academics and mental health diminished, support from friends and mentors of color on campus helped me successfully navigate these situations.

I began my first book, *Letters to My Sisters & Brothers: Practical Advice to Successfully Navigate Academia as a Student of Color*, using my doctoral research to help Black, Indigenous, and People of Color (BIPOC) students navigate higher education. Because of my hectic schedule, I stopped working on it for months. Spring 2020 changed that. The murders of Breonna Taylor, Ahmaud Arbery, and George Floyd amid the COVID-19 pandemic, which disproportionately affected Black, Brown, and Asian communities, had a deep impact on me. These twin traumas left me feeling defeated, depressed, and hopeless about transforming racism and other forms of societal oppression. Through this pain, I found my way back to the book. Working on the project became a form of self-care. It motivated me to get up each day, healed some of my wounds stemming from racism, and provided much needed encouragement to keep moving forward.

Letters to My Sisters & Brothers contains survey responses from undergraduate and graduate students of color across the United States. Asked to provide advice to incoming BIPOC students on how to navigate higher education, these students offered insight, experiences, and encouragement. The end of each section contains an activity created to better put their advice into practice.

To assist and encourage you on your publishing journey, here are the five steps I used to write my first book.

Start with Self-Affirmations

Self-affirmations are a great way to center yourself and begin the writing process. They remind you why you are writing, keep you focused on your work, and aid in remembering the importance of your distinctive story. A self-affirmation I used to write my book was:

> I am uniquely positioned to write this book. Many students of color will benefit from what I have to say. I will utilize my inner strength and perseverance to publish this book and make it a success.

I encourage you to write your own self-affirmation and post it somewhere you can see it each time you write (e.g., computer or desk).

Draw on Community Strength

When I felt discouraged or doubted my ability to complete the book, I reflected upon the strengths of my ancestors as well as BIPOC students' communal need for my message. Doing this each time I prepared to write gave me determination to create a unique resource that promotes holistic health and wellbeing.

In writing your book, think about the communities for which you are writing and what influence you want to have on them. Let this consideration guide your process to achieve your goals.

Implement Blocks of Dedicated Writing Time

One of the best strategies to finish writing your book is to build a daily writing regimen. Implementing dedicated blocks of writing time will help you attain this goal. For example, commit to write an hour every day in a distraction-free environment. It is important to treat this time as you would a job or other high-priority matter. Do not schedule other activities during this time or sit in an environment that is full of interruptions. To maximize your efforts and complete your book in a timely manner, schedule and adhere to dedicated writing time.

Use Audio Dictation

One reason people get stuck writing a book is the daunting and anxiety-provoking task of typing the entire manuscript. One way to overcome this obstacle is to audio dictate your book. Most computers and phones have dictation software that allows you to speak your book and it types for you. This strategy alleviates the pressure of typing, allows your ideas and words to flow, and minimizes perfectionism syndrome by eliminating editing while writing.

Solicit Feedback from Trusted Friends and Family

You can only get so far in life by yourself, and writing a book is no different. Getting feedback from trusted friends and family is a crucial part of writing a great book. Having people talk through ideas, read drafts, and give you critical, yet supportive, feedback will improve your writing immensely. It is natural to feel nervous about sharing your unfinished or "imperfect" work with others, but leaning into that fear will cause you to delay your writing. That same fear might stand in the way of completing your book to become a published author.

I hope my story and tips assist you in realizing your writing goals. Remember: the story you have to tell can only be told by you, and the story wants to be told through you.

Nelson O. O. Zounlome, Ph.D., is an author, scholar, and assistant professor of counseling psychology at the University of Kentucky. His research focuses on academic persistence and mental wellness to promote holistic healing among Black, Indigenous, and People of Color (BIPOC). Dr. Nelson authored *Letters to My Sisters & Brothers: Practical Advice to Successfully Navigate Academia as a Student of Color*, a workbook designed with culturally relevant advice and evidence-based exercises to help students of color thrive. He is also a mental health and academic thrive consultant through his company, Liberate the Block, which is dedicated to helping BIPOC communities liberate themselves to achieve their dreams.

Connect with Dr. Nelson
LiberateTheBlock.com
Facebook.com/Nelson.Zounlome
Linkedin.com/in/nelson-o-o-zounlome-3629081b6
Twitter.com/Nooz25

Dr. Nelson's Favorite Resource
Deep Work by Cal Newport because it helped him create a writing habit that allowed him to finish his book.

_____

_____

_____

_____

_____

_____

_____

_____

_____

_____

_____

_____

_____

_____

_____

_____

_____

_____

Oh, to Be a Writer Editors Love

Wendy Hart Beckman

Congratulations! You have written a book! The next thing that you should think about doing is getting an editor. If you intend to publish your book through a traditional (also called "commercial") publisher, you usually don't have to hire your own editor. If you have an agent, s/he might act as an editor for you.

Types of Editors

There are several types of editors, but most writers only deal with four or five of those types. They are as follows:

1. Acquisitions
2. Developmental
3. Content/substantive
4. Copy
5. Proofreader

Acquisitions editors are found in publishing houses. They are pitched by the author who either has an idea for a nonfiction book or a complete manuscript of a novel. These editors go to the editorial board to get your project accepted. If your idea is accepted, then the acquisitions editor discusses payment with you and/or your agent.

Note: Authors who are self-publishing usually do not deal with this type of editor.

Developmental editors work with authors to develop ideas for the book. Developmental editors often work with authors who have not written anything yet or have only prepared an outline. In traditional publishing, this role might also be managed by the acquisitions editor. In self-publishing, this type of editor might be called a "coach" or "book doctor." Book doctors and developmental editors need good people skills and the willingness to change someone's "baby." I am not willing to do that. One reason is that more than twenty years ago, I worked with an author whom I respected to get my novel manuscript in shape. By the time this person was through, my book had totally changed and was no longer mine. My decision was finalized when I realized that I had published more books than she had!

Content/substantive editors check for overall content, organization, and flow. This level of editor is looking at the chapter and paragraph level for problems with consistency or transitions. When I was about ten years old, my mother worked for an author and often typed her manuscripts (on a typewriter, not a computer). She had me read the manuscripts to catch mistakes. My great achievement was when I caught that the author had changed the main character's hair and eye color — and this was back in the day before men bleached their hair or before anyone wore fancy contact lenses to change eye color.

For this reason, content editors need to see the whole document at one time, if possible.

Copyeditors must see the entire document because they make sure that it is consistent in word choices, tone, structure, and other things. The copyeditor makes sure that tables are presented appropriately, and acronyms are spelled out on the first use. The copyeditor might check the Table of Contents against the chapters for order and wording. We think of copyeditors as looking at the line level of editing.

Proofreaders look at the manuscript word by word, punctuation mark by punctuation mark. Proofreaders should catch if the style of quotation marks changed from "curly" to straight, for example. What I do for my clients is a combination of content editing, copy editing, and proofreading.

The "Power" Relationship

When you're working with an editor of any kind, it is important to recognize who is in the power position. If you met former President Obama, you would probably give him more respect than if you met the new crossing guard at your child's school. You would treat both with respect, but you would probably be more deferential toward Mr. Obama.

In traditional publishing, the editor is in the power position. The editor is in charge of judgment calls, like what style guide is to be followed, what the cover will look like, even the title of the book! The author is not in charge. This fact is surprising to many authors who are new to traditional publishing. Some editors are nice and will seek your input—but they don't have to! The editor of my first book wanted to title it *Pioneers of the Harlem Renaissance*. I was nervous about speaking up, but I reminded her that the audience was fifth to seventh graders who can be very literal. I didn't want them to be waiting for Conestoga wagons. In my third book, *Dating, Relationships, and Sexuality: What Teens Should Know*, I wanted to start one chapter with this stark statement: "If you have unprotected sex, even just once, be prepared to be a parent in nine months or to contract a disease from which you may never recover." The editor said that it was too gloomy and insisted that I remove it. If I had self-published, I would have kept it. Remember: editors are usually great people, but the publishing house pays their salary, so it is the company (especially the sales department) who often has more influence than the author. Of course, if you're the next Toni Morrison, Nova Roberts, or Maya Angelou, you have more control over your books than when you are a new author.

In self-publishing, the author is in the power position because the smart author *hired* the editor. In this relationship, the author is in charge of judgment calls. For example, will the book be in first or third person? Will the author use his or her own name or a pseudonym? The editor is in charge of what is correct/incorrect. For example, "I am going to lie down for a nap" is correct. "I am going to lay down for a nap" is incorrect, and it is always incorrect in that context. Periods and commas (in the United States) go inside quotation marks, without exception, no matter what your grade school teacher told you. In self-publishing, the author usually pays the editor. I do lots of editing for a woman who publishes other people's books. (Note: This type of publisher used to be called a book producer or book packager, but those terms are not used as commonly. Because service providers refer to themselves as "publishers," it is more difficult to tell the difference between self-publishing and traditional publishing houses. The biggest clue: the writer never pays a traditional publishing house.) She pays me to edit and then puts my fee in her bill to her clients. I don't directly interact with her clients at all.

What Authors Should Do Before the Manuscript Goes to the Editor

A current trend in self-publishing is to "talk through" the publication—whether it is one article, one story, or a whole book—and record it. This recording is then transcribed by a typist, publisher, author, or transcription software. Voilà! Instant manuscript! This manuscript, however, is a very rough draft. The author should do at least two things before turning the manuscript over to any editor: read the manuscript through (preferably out loud) and run it through a spell check.

I have edited manuscripts for clients who could have saved themselves a chunk of money if they had done this before giving it to me. Don't give the proofreader your rough draft! I recently edited a manuscript for a woman who had gone this route. Many of her mistakes were words that sounded the same as or similar to the intended word. Where she had dictated "voilà," the transcriber had typed "wahlah." Where the author had said "ink pen," the transcriber had typed "ink pin." You can see how transcription software or someone listening to a recording and typing a manuscript could mistake these words. Upon reading it, however, the author should have had an easy time catching these slips. Also, since I am a copyeditor and proofreader, mine should be almost the last set of hands to touch the manuscript. Don't give the proofed manuscript to your child's teacher to read after it's been edited. Once your manuscript is professionally proofed, no one else should touch it.

Always do a spell check before you pass your manuscript to anyone. However, don't assume spell check is correct; it is often wrong. For example, spell check often prompts me to add an apostrophe to plurals. This is wrong, unless you're making a plural of an acronym, a letter, or a number. Spell check, however, is a good set of first "eyes."

Proofread your manuscript by reading it out loud to yourself. Every mistake you find and fix on your own saves you money and keeps traditional publishing editors happy.

Things That Authors Often Don't Check

When I see certain things in a manuscript, my antennae go up. Writers usually don't invent new mistakes and often repeat those of my other clients. I spend lots of time on Bible references. Even if you've been a pastor for forty years, if you're quoting the Bible, don't go by memory. Get the words right. BibleGateway.com and BibleHub.com are helpful for verifying translations.

Sometimes the problem is not your memory; sometimes the Bible translations are inconsistent. For example, Matthew 18:22 is inconsistent among the various translations. Here are two of the most commonly used versions. Note the difference (emphasis mine):

- *New King James Version*: Jesus said to him, "I do not say to you, up to seven times, but up to **seventy times seven**.

- *New American Standard Bible:* Jesus said to him, "I do not say to you, up to seven times, but up to **seventy-seven** times.

Don't assume something comes from the Bible. It might not, such as "Cleanliness is next to godliness." That comes from the "Bible" or "Gospel" of your mother!

Note what translation you're using after each quote. However, if you *always* use the same translation, or if you usually use the same translation, you can cite it once at the beginning, then just cite exceptions, if there are any. If you mix up the versions in one quote, just note that it is paraphrased. For example, let's say that your favorite translation of Psalm 23 is the *New King James Version*, but you like the way the *New American Standard Bible* says "lets" instead of "makes."

- *New King James Version:* He makes me to lie down in green pastures; He leads me beside the still waters.
- *New American Standard Bible:* He lets me lie down in green pastures; He leads me beside quiet waters.

You might write it like this:

He lets me lie down in green pastures; He leads me beside the still waters. (paraphrased)

Quoting the Work of Others

Sometimes your editor can save your wallet. Let's say that you want to quote a song in your manuscript. If it was published before 1924, it is probably in the public domain, which means that you can use it freely. Check anyway. You should still give appropriate credit, though. However, if the song was written more recently, it is copyrighted. You cannot use *even one line* of the lyrics unless you have permission. If you don't get permission, you run the risk of being successfully sued. The "Fair Use" Clause permits writers to use quotes for educational or critique purposes, but it is not *carte blanche* to quote people's work at will just because you're a teacher.

It's complicated, but it boils down to whether your work infringes on their ability to make a profit.

Also, don't assume that the person (or group) who made the song famous is the composer or lyricist. For example, Whitney Houston did not write "I Will Always Love You," Dolly Parton did. Manfred Mann did not write "Blinded by the Light," Bruce Springsteen did. Online lyric websites don't always cite the correct creator and often violate the copyright laws themselves. If you're quoting poems or famous quotes, again, verify who actually said it. For example, what famous person said, "We should ask what we can do for our country?" John F. Kennedy? Yes, but others expressed the idea first. In 1884, Oliver Wendell Holmes said, "We pause to become conscious of our national life and to rejoice in it, to recall **what our country has done for us, and to ask ourselves what we can do for our country** in return." The Kennedys were very well-educated, so in their speeches they often identified whom they were quoting. History has often omitted these notes made in the margin.

Don't assume if the online version of something says "Anonymous" that it really is. The "Serenity Prayer," for example, was written by theologian Reinhold Niebuhr, not Anonymous. Five minutes of searching on the internet will pick this up. Your editor might already know it, too.

Finding a Freelance Editor

If you're looking for an editor, word of mouth is always the best. Ask your publisher or writer friends whom they use. Once you get some names, then make sure the person is a good fit for you.

Ask the editor if s/he prefers hard copy or digital. Ask the editor how s/he gives feedback. One way is by using "Track Changes" on the digital copy to make suggestions or fix everything. You'll want to establish ahead of time whether you want the editor to fix anything s/he finds or just flag whatever s/he finds. If you give your editor a printed copy, then the only option is to mark up the hard copy.

Ask the editor what s/he marks up. Here's what I do. First, I fix outright mistakes, like "laying" for "lying." Mistakes or clear errors are not up for discussion. I will call my client's attention to inconsistencies or where the author has a choice. For example, a character might be called "Mat" on some pages but "Matt" on others. Which way does the author want it to be? Or a character might start using words that are inconsistent with how the author has presented that character. I will flag (or highlight) and make suggestions on things that require a thoughtful decision by the author. For example, I recently read a middle-grade book (intended for the eleven-to-thirteen-year-old reader) that toward the end started dropping the F-bomb. This is usually frowned upon.

If the editor you're considering hiring has given you all the "right" answers so far, ask if s/he is willing to edit three to five pages for a trial. Many editors will not charge for this sample, which gives you both a chance to see if you will like working together.

How to Deal with the Editor's Feedback

First, see "The 'Power' Relationship," above. Don't take revision suggestions personally and react with ego. Revisions are not rejections. Read the whole document and note things that you want to discuss with the editor. Most editors will go over comments or corrections that the author doesn't understand. You have to respect the editor's time, however. Don't make several calls. If the editor has a "day job," don't call the editor at that day job. Send a text or email and ask for the editor to call you.

After being a freelance editor for a couple of decades, I have put a higher value on my time. I will discuss the comments for thirty minutes, total. After that, I start billing at my full rate.

Pay the editor. I had a client who was a late payer (several months went by). When I reluctantly accepted another job from this same client, I asked for payment before I sent her the edited manuscript. She had her niece call me to see why I was holding her manuscript hostage. When I explained to the niece what the problem was, she laughed and paid me. Meanwhile, the author burned that bridge. I declined all future editing requests.

Finally, learn from the editor's feedback. If you send another manuscript to the same editor and make the same mistakes that you made in the first one, don't expect the editor to be happy about it. When you get the marked-up copy, review what the editor fixed so you can learn from it.

Remember, editors want to help you get published, especially if you thank them in your book. Any time I see one of my clients' books in print, I feel like a proud grandmother!

Final words of advice: make sure you spell "foreword" and/or "acknowledgments" correctly. Editors don't often see these front-matter pages. You don't want your editor to cringe when he/she gets thanked.

Wendy Hart Beckman is an award-winning writer and editor. She has published more than 300 articles in print and online publications and has received a baker's dozen of awards for her writing, editing, and desktop publishing. Her last four books focused on the history of Cincinnati, where she has lived for forty-one years. (But she still thinks of Stockbridge, Massachusetts, as "home.") Wendy's bachelor's degrees are in geology and natural science/technical communications from Virginia Tech and the University of Cincinnati, respectively. She has a master's degree in English/editing and publishing and a graduate certificate in professional writing from UC. Wendy has taught business, scientific, and technical writing at UC, and cultural diversity at Miami University. She is a full-time writer and freelance editor. Wendy is the mother of three sons, wife to Steve, and grandmother to one adorable granddaughter (with another grand on the way).

Connect with Wendy
WendyOnWriting.com
Facebook.com/Wendy.Beckman
Twitter.com/beckcomm

Wendy's Favorite Resource
The Online Writing Lab of Purdue University, https://owl.purdue.edu.

Why You Need a Great Book Editor

Susan Mary Malone

Did I just see your eyes glaze over? You already *know* you need an editor for your work, no matter which publishing venue you're pursuing. This has been beaten into your head (hopefully not literally) to the point where you, yourself, tell this to others. This subject has been discussed to the moon and back, so I'm sure you're well versed in the reasons you need a book editor.

But you may not realize the most important one.

What seems the First Stage is actually the Last

The last thing you want to do is send a book out into the world full of typos, grammatical issues, and spelling problems. Yes, yes, we all know this. A hard copy-edit and final proofing are mandatory before you publish. They are, however, the very *last* steps in the process. Before you get here, so much editing, revising, and rewriting, and more editing and revising and rewriting has already been done. Right?

So, let's discuss what you already *know* on this subject, but do a bit of a deeper dive.

Stick with me for a minute, and then we'll get to the main reason you need a great book editor.

Beware of Bad Advice

As you're starting into this crazy creative endeavor, it's difficult to know who to believe. But, even once you're down the road a bit, getting too much advice is like having too many proverbial cooks in the kitchen. Everybody uses different seasonings, and if you dump them all in, oh, my, what a hot mess.

And that's if you're getting critique from folks who've been in the trenches a while. Because the old adage of "you can't know what you don't yet know" applies here as well. Writers contact me often, saying that writing sites and articles are so confusing. They often find diametrically opposed veins of advice from folks who are supposed to know what they're doing.

I will take a wildly unpopular side here — *most of the time, it's the blind leading the blind.* So, proceed with utmost caution through this mine-filled maze.

And even in one's early stages of writing, the twelve-step motto works: "Take what you need and leave the rest." Of course, in those early stages, it's tough to separate the wheat from the chaff. But you'll get there!

The big surge of beta readers is all the rage now as well. And while that can be helpful, even established authors can only be of so much help unless they're editors themselves. Identifying that something is wrong is a far cry from knowing different options to fix it. Much less being able to teach you the skills needed to do so.

I've also known lots of writers to avail themselves of beta readers with their manuscripts. Send it to ten folks; you most often get ten vastly different takes on it. So, which do you listen to? Even that bestselling author may give you bad advice.

I've seen quite terrible advice come from beta readers. So, it's not something I advise.

Using your close friends/family as first readers is most often worse. They truly can't be objective. And you know what's funny? Most times, they're actually harder on you than necessary. Go figure. But they have no clue about what makes for a good book, except that they liked it or didn't.

The Beginning

To begin, a good editor will help you <u>tighten your prose</u> until it sings, uncovering the beauty that is your true voice. This is trickier than it might sound. A writer's voice evolves as s/he goes, often beginning with clunky prose then growing ever more flowing and smoother with each paragraph/scene/chapter written. It just takes time to hone it down to uniquely yours. Where someone reading a book says, "Oh, that's Toni Morrison's voice. I'd know it anywhere."

*This stage is vital. Nothing — and I mean nothing — can be allowed to get in the way of **you** finding and perfecting your voice.*

I've heard from many writers that their editors have revised in the *editor's* voice — not the *writer's*. You cannot imagine how often I hear this. And it makes me cringe.

Just know that this is a travesty of the highest order. The editor's job *isn't* to change your voice or rewrite for you. That's a ghostwriter. But the thing is, even a ghost needs to sound like the actual person who hired her. The task at hand is to help you polish *your own* voice, again, until it sings off the pages.

The thing is, polishing that prose while maintaining the <u>writer's voice</u> must be done with great care.

And every bit as important, to teach you the tools of why, where, and how so you'll own those tools for your lifetime. If you don't know why something was changed, how can you even learn from it?

But all of this is still not why you need a great book editor.

Diving Deeper into the Substance

Getting into the meat of things, a great editor helps you <u>uncover your characters</u>, helps you deepen them, and find their flaws and virtues. Keep in mind, this must mirror what the protagonist has to face *in* the story. The inner world always mirrors the outer world in great fiction. That melds the characters with the plot ensuring the book is all of one piece.

Developing characters so that they jump off the page proves a daunting challenge. What may be oh-so clear in your head might have gotten lost in translation. A said editor will help you enormously in accomplishing this feat. Employ one who utilizes exercises to help draw the essence of your characters from you so that, in the end, your reader knows them as well as you do.

Tying all this to a tightly woven plot, which follows the true <u>arc of the storyline</u>, can cause you to yank out every hair on your head. But that's where a good editor comes in as well. They should help you streamline the action and show where breathers for your characters (and your readers) need to come in. And cut away the superfluous and expand upon what truly matters. These tasks will then leave you (and your readers) with a definite beginning, middle, and end, with characters who change and grow, satisfying on all counts.

Yes, all tricky indeed. But still not the main reason you need a great book editor.

The Wind Tunnel of Revision

So finally, you're into that <u>revision</u>, which itself can be so overwhelming, especially at first. Once you get your edited manuscript and in-depth critique back from your editor, the first-blush response is always, "OMG! There's so much to do! Where do I even start?"

I hear this often. :)

Because *real books* — not the ones just tossed out there — take *lots* of revision. And revision *is* rewriting, not just polishing, for even established authors. That beautiful vision you had, that heady blast of inspiration? It most likely went sprawling in a plethora of diverse directions and far away from the mainstream. Which is absolutely fine! That's why God invented revision in the first place. There is almost always lots of cutting and lots of adding as well. Lots of fleshing-out folks (characters) and lots of scaling some back. Much cutting off of threads that go nowhere. Remember, all streams must end up back into the mainstream of the book. No matter how beautiful that scene is, you now have to ax. Lots of building bridges where leaps were taken over a wide crevasse.

Getting started into revision can be halting. The most vital job your editor does after the first edit is to be your sounding board. As you bounce back and forth with the editor while going through revisions, you may have your hands full with other tasks:

- Diving in and grappling to learn a new tool
- Ensuring your characters are coming to life
- Wondering if your plot is moving at a good pace

Therefore, nothing—*absolutely nothing*—beats having that person in your corner. You've chosen a trusted voice in this industry for your editor, and s/he knows the ins and outs of making a good book great. You must have confidence in your editor's abilities, or you need a new one! Having them point out where you're still falling down and how to fix it is priceless.

Confidence is hard-won when writing books. First, it takes a while treading water in those roiling seas, being bashed by every stinking wave that crests over you. Then, feeling the sharks nipping at your toes before you can traverse that ocean like Diana Nyad, the American distance swimmer and journalist. In

2013, she became the first person to complete a swim from Cuba to Florida without the protection of a shark cage. Now that's confidence and courage!

This leads us to:

The Deeper Reason You Need a Great Book Editor

We're an odd and fragile group, those of us who create. I've yet to meet a writer who doesn't face insecurities about his or her work. But, as I often say, the gene for creating fiction has on its flip side the gene for doubt. It just comes with the territory — no matter how much you've published.

And it can be difficult to find your sea legs, especially for the first few books. I have NY *Times* bestselling authors who still contact me and say, "Would you look at the setup, so I know I'm on track?" We all need a confidence boost now and then.

The point being, as I often say, *writing well and for publication just isn't learned in a vacuum.*

While the initial creating and revision must be done in that quiet, hopefully, well-lit room, after that, you have to inch your way with it to the outside world. Which we often do by peeking around the doorframe and seeing what bloody fanged monsters wait at the ready to devour our very babies. We slam the door! Bolt the locks. Take a deep breath. Still ourselves. Cautiously, crack it open again. Finally, dig down to find the courage to walk that book out into the sunlight.

Those who haven't written think we're nuts. Those who have understand entirely.

<u>A great editor is your cheerleader</u>. One who keeps telling you that you truly *can* do this, despite the pitfalls. One who believes in *you* and *your* book and who urges you on.

A great editor not only helps you produce the very best book yours can be, but holds your hand through the process, so you don't drown in the crazy sea of publishing. There is no substitute for bouncing off ideas to someone who knows your story and characters in an endeavor mainly done in solitary confinement.

The very essence of why you need a great editor is to help you build your confidence.

Not with airy-fairy platitudes, not with "anybody can write a book" (which trust me, they can't, for various reasons), but with actual publishing-world knowledge.

Writing for publication is a difficult task. It will humble you to your knees. But, you know, we're not trying to sell bread dough here or any other "outside" product. Instead, in creating fiction, or even narrative nonfiction, you're exposing pieces of your heart and soul. It doesn't matter how far down the line you are, how many books you've written, the people, the places, the events, well, they're all part of *you*.

I'll never forget when my first book was about to be published, and I was reviewing the galleys. In the middle of the night, I woke up in a cold sweat, thinking, *my mother's friends are going to read this!* Talk about panic. Of course, they ultimately did. And it wasn't always pretty. But by then, I believed in the book so strongly (I had a fabulous editor to cheer me on), it wasn't an issue.

I bet you've had some variation on that theme. This is your baby and, more deeply, your very womb of creation as well — all vital parts of you.

I can tell you this for a fact: Every single writer I've ever worked with, who is willing to truly dive in and learn this craft, who bounces off of me as s/he goes, who faces the heartache, the rejection, the blood, sweat, and tears of getting a book ready for publication, everyone has felt confident in the end that this is the very best book s/he could produce. At least for now.

And another secret? *Talent* is often misunderstood. I've worked with writers with boatloads of talent who weren't willing to put in the herculean effort to learn, dig in, learn again, dig deeper, and finally scale that mountain to write a successful book. Conversely, I've worked with even more writers whose talent at the onset was hidden, but I could see pieces of it. Who then did all that work, and oh my stars — their talents just shone for the world to see.

I firmly believe if you have the desire, the talent is there within you. A great editor will help you bring it out in the form of a beautiful book. And even more — will instill that confidence in you, the author, so that even when doubts arise (which they will), you'll have a touchstone to soothe that midnight terror.

When that editor tells you that your book is ready to go, it's ready to go. And you can not only take that to the bank, but you can also sleep at night without fear.

Texas native, Susan Mary Malone, has published two novels, a collection of short stories, co-authored four nonfiction books, and sold more short stories than she can count. As a highly successful book editor, fifty-plus Malone-edited books have sold to traditional publishers. Many have received prestigious literary awards; one was made into a *Hallmark Hall of Fame* film (another is in production). Her own stories revolve around the passion and purpose, the myths and meaning in women's lives. With dual passions of writing and editing, she feels extremely grateful to live in a world of words.

Connect with Susan
MaloneEditorial.com
Facebook.com/maloneeditorial
Linkedin.com/in/maloneeditorialservices

Susan's Favorite Resource
The Writer's Journey by Christopher Vogler because it is the best roadmap for entwining the characters with the plot.

Celebrate Your Success

Valerie J. Lewis Coleman

We are serious about helping you land paid speaking engagements, media attention, and book sales. Contact me at info@penofthewriter.com with the book you published using *Do It Right the First Time* as your resource. Your book will be

- Included in an eblast to my 30,000+ fans, friends, and followers.
- Listed on the Pen of the Writer (POWER) Wall of Fame.
- Entered for the Do It Right Bestseller where the top-selling title will be acknowledged each year.

Plus, I'll host a live panel-style interview to further magnify and monetize your message.

I want to serve more aspiring authors to achieve their publishing dreams and I need your help. Can you do me a favor?

- Email me a testimonial about your experience with *Do It Right the First Time*. I'll share it on social media and my Google business page with a link to your site.
- Post on social media tagging me and the authors whose contributions helped you most. Use hashtags: #DoItRightTheFirstTime, #PenOfTheWriter, and #SelfPublishing to create a viral thread.

- Write an Amazon review at https://amzn.to/3zeQ51j. As Carolyn Howard-Johnson explained in *Do It Right the First Time: Conversations with Marketing Experts*, your reviews hyperlink back to your author page.

Congrats in advance!

Your Bestseller Resources

"If there's a book that you want to read, but
it hasn't been written yet,
then you must write it."
— Toni Morrison

Valerie J. Lewis Coleman

Writing Resources

Talk with Val	https://penofthewriter.as.me
Checklists & Guides	Email <u>info@penofthewriter.com</u> for • Pen of the Writer's Weekly Planning Calendar and • Write Your Bestseller Checklist *421 Ways to Say Said? Simplify Dialogue* https://www.nownovel.com/blog/ways-to-say-said-simplify-dialogue *Cheat Sheets for Writing Body Language* https://www.writerswrite.co.za/cheat-sheets-for-writing-body-language
Streaming Music	Pandora.com Spotify.com
Organizing	EverNote.com Scrivener.com
Time Management	Clockify.me
Transcription	Dragon Software Cloud.Google.com/speech-to-text Otter.ai Reedsy.com
Verify Scriptures	BibleGateway.com BibleHub.com

Writing Assistance	Grammarly.com HemingwayApp.com LoreStorytelling.com Owl.Purdue.edu ProWritingAid.com TheCreativePenn.com TheMoth.org
Writing Events	FlourishWritersAcademy.com FreeYourMindWritersRetreat.com
Writing Groups	Facebook.com/groups/ FreeYourMindWritersClub GeorgiaWriters.org

_____

_____

_____

_____

_____

_____

_____

_____

_____

Books on Writing

Title	Author
Bird by Bird: Some Instructions on Writing and Life	Anne Lamott
The Christian Writer's Manual of Style	Robert Hudson
Deep Work	Cal Newport
How to Write a Children's Fiction Book	Karen Cioffi
On Writing: A Memoir of the Craft	Stephen King
Self-Publishing Made Easy: Passionate Writing https://bit.ly/3m72rA8 (case sensitive)	Valerie J. Lewis Coleman
The Writer's Journey	Christopher Vogler
Writers Market	Writer's DigestEditors

For emotional clarity, connect with Chanelle Wilson. She is a licensed emotional polarity technique (EPT) practitioner who helps you find it, fix it, and forgive it. Contact her at 937.396.2230 or gutfeelingworks@gmail.com.

Valerie J. Lewis Coleman

144

_____

_____

_____

_____

_____

_____

_____

_____

_____

_____

_____

_____

_____

_____

_____

_____

_____

_____

_____

_____

Valerie J. Lewis Coleman